Welcome Home
Timeless Truth | Unhurried Focus

Written by
Chris Wall | Chad Balthrop | Paul Purifoy
Brent Andrews | Keith Davis | Brad Aylor

With family materials written by
Susan Helm | Kelly Wehunt | Grant Collins

Inspired by "My Heart - Christ's Home" by Robert Boyd Munger

First Baptist Church of Owasso

Welcome Home
Copyright © 2015 by First Baptist Church of Owasso
ISBN 978-1-329-74998-6

Published by First Baptist Church of Owasso
PO BOX 1020
Owasso, OK 74055
(918) 272-2294 | fbcowasso.org

All Scritpure quotations, unless otherwise indicated, are taken from the Holy Bible, New Kings James Version. Copyright © 1982.

"My Heart - Christ's Home" by Robert Boyd Munger.

"Lord, make me to know my end, and what is the measure of my days, that I may know how frail I am. Indeed, You have made my days as handbreadths, and my age is as nothing before You; certainly every man at his best state is but vapor. Surely every man walks about like a shadow; surely they busy themselves in vain; he heaps up riches, and does not know who will gather them."

Psalm 39:4 – 6

contents

The 'B' Badge of Honor

"I'm late! I'm late! For a very important date! No time to say hello, goodbye, I'M LATE, I'M LATE, I'M LATE!"

—Alice in Wonderland

You remember the tale. There sits Alice next to a tree when the White Rabbit comes charging by, hurried in speech and mannerisms, looking at his watch and harried in appearance. He must be important. He's well dressed. He has somewhere to be. And he's made it clear, "HE'S LATE!" So down the rabbit hole he goes. To quote the book:

> "...Alice started to her feet, for it flashed across her mind that she had never before seen a rabbit with either a waistcoat-pocket, or a watch to take it out of, and burning with curiosity, she ran across the field after it, and was just in time to see it pop down a large rabbit-hole under the hedge. In another moment down went Alice after it, *never once considering how in the world she was to get out again.*"

There is a badge of honor worn by people today. We flaunt it in front of friends and coworkers. We flash it like a Monopoly card, "Get Out of Anything Free". We parade around

1

with it and show it to our family, when we have time for family. It is our excuse to be abrupt with people, rude to some and dismissive of others. We may not be wealthy. We may not be influential. The career we've chosen may not change the world. But we are BUSY – and therein we find our significance.

Like Alice charging down the rabbit-hole we fill our time with stuff to do, places to be, things to see, and we often do this, "…never once considering how in the world we are to get out again." Busyness is the popular and accepted addiction of our modern world. There are so many good things to do, so many different ways to do them, and only so many hours in the day. The

*The challenge for today is not, '**WHAT** can I do?' but '**WHERE** do I start!?'*

challenge for today is not, 'WHAT can I do?' but 'WHERE do I start!?' So, how do I choose what's best for family, my friends, and me? How do I find my part in the Kingdom of God?

Here's the deal – being BUSY is not the problem. Life happens. Jobs have to be done. Kids have to be raised. Parties need to be attended. Friends want to get together. Houses must be maintained. Parents have to be cared for. And through it all we struggle to build our lives on a foundation of faith in God, which involves church and Bible studies, volunteering, and serving. We're going to be busy. The true test is whether or not we're busy doing the things God has planned for us. Being busy doing something is not the same as being busy doing right things.

As I read the gospels I discover that Jesus was always busy. Yet His busyness was always the work of God. From eating a simple meal with 5000 of His closest friends to teaching eternal truth beside the Sea of Galilee,

Jesus was always busy but never frantic. He had the most significant of tasks to accomplish, yet was never rushed.

Here's what Jesus knew that we need to catch:

- Busy does not equal IMPORTANT.
- Busy does not equal RIGHT.
- Busy does not equal PRODUCTIVE.
- Busy does not equal LIFE.

Remember the story of Lazarus? Two sisters, one brother. Mary, Martha, and Lazarus. They would call Jesus more than a mentor. They would call Him friend. On many occasions after a long day of teaching, healing, and performing miracles, Jesus would end up back in their home. Martha was the best hostess in town; Mary, a faithful follower and Lazarus, a good friend. They had heard His teaching and seen the wonders He could work so when Lazarus became ill, their response was quick and confident. "We need Jesus." Mary and Martha sent messengers to Him.

Busy does not equal **LIFE**.

"Help us, Jesus. Come quickly, Lazarus is sick. You're our only hope."

Yet Jesus didn't come. Rather than drop what He was doing to run off and save a friend He does the most amazing thing. He waits. I think His response to the messengers is interesting. He doesn't tell Mary and Martha He's too busy to come – it's likely He was – instead He says, "This sickness will not end in death. It is for the glory of God, to bring glory to the Son of God." John 11:4 (NCV).

When was the last time you were asked to do something and you knew God's plan for your day so clearly that you could answer like this?

"I'm sorry. I can't do that right now. God's got a plan for me today. If I do that, I would really just be in the way."

Jesus waits. Lazarus dies.

I'm sure Mary and Martha were upset. When Jesus finally arrives, only Martha goes to greet Him. Mary, her faith shaken, simply stays home while Martha confronts Jesus. You can hear the disappointment in her voice,

What would your life be like if you weren't so busy?

"Why didn't you come? You could have fixed this." But Jesus kept His word and in His time and in His way, really in a way no one ever imagined, He 'heals' Lazarus by raising him from the dead! Jesus overcame the tyranny of the urgent and by doing so, accomplished His purpose in one place while performing a miracle and saving a friend in another.

What would your life be like if you weren't so busy doing 'stuff', but instead were busy doing those things clearly in God's plan for your day? What if your every choice led to positive, productive results? How would your days be different if you so clearly understood your purpose that the words you spoke and the actions you took would always add value to the people around you? How would this change your family? How would it affect your friends? Would your income change? Would your career path be different?

THE SEASON OF LENT

The season of Lent is an opportunity to slow down and consider how God's amazing grace influences you every day. Your life is full, but is it full with the things that matter most? For the next several weeks you will be encouraged to examine yourself in the light of Scripture.

Lent is about sacrifice. It's about giving up something

you love for something you love even more. For some, Lent is an opportunity to give more than you think you can afford as you trust God to provide. The goal is deeper than getting organized or simplifying your life. Lent is about removing those things that distract us from drawing close to God. This practice of Lent is called fasting. It's about reducing the noise that makes hearing God's voice difficult. It's about making time to slow down, pause, and focus your heart and mind on this remarkable, loving relationship God has given through the sacrifice of Jesus Christ.

AS WE BEGIN

Take a moment to stop and pray. Ask God to give you the wisdom and discernment you need to make right choices. Ask for the courage and strength to overcome those parts of your life that are out of balance and that keep you from living up to your God-given potential. Thank God for His care and concern for you and praise Him for the answers He will surely bring.

We find this promise in 2 Peter 1:3, "[God's] divine power has given us everything we need for life and godliness." (NIV). Your life doesn't have to be ruled by busyness. You have been given everything you need to have a life worth living, a life that honors God. You can start today. Stop parading your busyness around as though being busy means something. Don't settle for being busy doing just anything. Get busy doing right things. You'll find your 'to do' list done, your needs met, your relationships healthy, and interruptions – just another opportunity from God. We've already jumped down this rabbit-hole. While we're here let's draw close to God and busy ourselves with what matters most.

welcome home

God loves people.

God is the master builder. This profound truth is the foundation on which every believer builds their life.

"For I am persuaded that neither death nor life, nor angels nor principalities nor powers, nor things present nor things to come, nor height nor depth, nor any other created thing, shall be able to separate us from the love of God which is in Christ Jesus our Lord."

Romans 8:38-39

Sin hurts people.

We try to build a life apart from God. We rebel against His plans. We reject His principles, precepts, and practices. Mistakes are made. We sin not simply because of mistakes. We sin because we like it. Sin ravages our house. It breaks our relationship with God and ruins our relationship with others.

"For the wages of sin is death..."

Romans 6:23

Jesus died for my sin and rose from the dead.

The Master Builder has a master plan. He sent His one and only Son to prove His love for us, to renovate the home of our lives, and restore our relationship with the Heavenly Father. Jesus died for our sin because He was the only one who could. He rose from the dead because He followed the plans of the Master Builder to the letter. He shared those plans through His Word.

"In my Father's house are many mansions; if it were not so, I would have told you. I go to prepare a place for you. And if I go and prepare a place for you, I will come again and receive you to Myself; that where I am, there you may be also."

John 14:2-3

That's why I can be forgiven.

When we place our faith in Jesus Christ, our sin is forgiven. He takes up residence in our heart through the Holy Spirit. He applies the plans of the Master Builder to our lives and we are transformed by the goodness of His grace to the glory of His praise for the greatness of His name!

> *"I have been crucified with Christ; it is no longer I who live, but Christ lives in me; and the life which I now live in the flesh I live by faith in the Son of God, who loved me and gave Himself for me."*
>
> Galatians 2:20

With my heart, Christ's home, Jesus is the owner, designer, and builder of my life.

Yet there is a temptation to pick and choose which parts of our lives we surrender. We hold something back, as though the one we trust for eternal salvation can't be trusted with the details of our everyday lives.

For the next 6 weeks you will be challenged to examine the different rooms of the home in your heart. With Christ as the owner, designer, and builder of your life, you will consider the clutter, the unconfessed sin, and the unwilling surrender you may have stored up, held on to, or even tried to hide in your heart. You will be encouraged, through Scripture, to examine yourself, confess as needed, surrender or sacrifice as necessary, and discover the freedom that comes from resting in a deeper, more intimate relationship with God.

Think of it as an extreme home makeover…for your heart.

making a house, a home

THE HOUSE

Each chapter begins with the description of a room from Robert Boyd Munger's book, "*My Heart - Christ's Home*". Let the picture he paints of your life, through the house he describes, inspire your imagination as you consider how to draw close to God through this season of Lent.

WEEKLY MEMORY VERSE

You can't live God's Word if you don't know God's Word. The Weekly Memory Verse was selected to challenge, instruct, and encourage you as you examine your heart through the lens of Scriptures during the season of Lent and beyond.

DAILY DEVOTIONAL

Five devotions have been written for each week. These devotions follow a simple pattern, S.O.A.P. - Scripture. Observation. Application. Prayer.

Make time each day to read the Scriptures, observe, and apply what it says, and then pray it back to God. On day six, write your own short S.O.A.P. devotion about that week's memory verse. On day seven, review what you've learned throughout the week.

CHALLENGE TO FAST

The challenge to fast is the spiritual discipline that helps every believer learn self control. But more than this, fasting helps us remove the distractions that prevent us from giving God our undivided attention.

Each week you'll be challenged to fast from something specific. Fasting shouldn't be easy. If the suggested fast isn't challenging, choose something that is. Fasting should stretch your faith, challenge your self control, and draw you into a deeper relationship with God.

WITH YOUR FAMILY

Throughout the season of Lent, the things you discover about yourself and your relationship with God may be quite personal. You may want to protect the privacy of your devotions.

You were designed for community. God has given you a family. He's blessed you with friends. You are surrounded by other believers who are also growing in their journey of faith. Use the Family Section to encourage conversations about these devotions with your entire family.

week one

MY HEART - CHRIST'S HOME

One evening I invited Jesus Christ into my heart. What an entrance He made! It was not a spectacular, emotional thing, but very real. Something happened at the very center of my life. He came into the darkness of my heart and turned on the light. He built a fire on the hearth and banished the chill. He started music where there had been silence. He filled the emptiness with His own loving, wonderful fellowship. I have never regretted opening the door to Christ and I never will.

In the joy of this new relationship I said to Jesus Christ, "Lord, I want this heart of mine to be Yours. I want to have You settle down here and be perfectly at home. Everything that I have belongs to You. Let me show You around."

THE STUDY

The first room was the study—the library. In my home this room of the mind is a very small room with very thick walls. But it is a very important room. In a sense it is the control room of the house. He entered with me and looked around at the books on the bookcase, the magazines upon the table, and the pictures on the walls. As I followed His gaze I became uncomfortable.

Strangely, I had not felt self-conscious about this before, but now that He was there looking at these things I was embarrassed. Some books were there that His eyes were too pure to behold. On the table were a few magazines that a Christian had no business reading. As for the pictures on the walls—the imaginations and thoughts of the mind—some of these were shameful.

Red-faced, I turned to Him and said, "Master, I know that this room needs to be cleaned up and made over. Will You help me make it what it ought to be?"

"Certainly!" He said. "I'm glad to help you. First of all, take all the things that you are reading and looking at which are not helpful, pure, good and true, and throw them out! Now put on the empty shelves the books of the Bible. Fill the library with Scripture and meditate on it day and night. As for the pictures on the walls, you will have difficulty controlling these images, but I have something that will help." He gave me a full-size portrait of Himself. "Hang this centrally," He said, "on the wall of the mind."

FAST THIS WEEK

What will you remove this week from "The Study" of your life so that you might better focus your heart and mind on God?

This week, take time away from media. Don't watch TV or movies. Use the internet, email, apps, your phone, any books or magazines only for necessary business rather than for entertainment. Replace your unhurried, relaxed moments with genuine rest, time with family, and time reading the Word of God and praying to Him.

THIS WEEK'S MEMORY VERSE

"I have been crucified with Christ; it is no longer I who live, but Christ lives in me; and the life which I now live in the flesh I live by faith in the Son of God, who loved me and gave Himself for me."

Galatians 2:20

SCRIPTURE

Read Galatians 5

Focus -

"So I say, walk by the Spirit, and you will not gratify the desires of the flesh. For the flesh desires what is contrary to the Spirit, and the Spirit what is contrary to the flesh. They are in conflict with each other, so that you are not to do whatever you want. But if you are led by the Spirit, you are not under the law."

Galatians 5:16-18

OBSERVATION

"Walking" is a common idea in scripture that communicates the way a person lives and conducts his or her life. As we turn our attention to those inner characteristics of the mind and heart, most often, our walk is a natural reflection of the innermost focus of our heart. To "walk by the Spirit" means to be under the constant, moment-by-moment direction, control, and guidance of the Spirit of God. From the moment of salvation, the Holy Spirit has moved into your life and gives you the faithful voice of conviction to listen to His direction over every other competing pressure.

week one

APPLICATION

Take a few minutes and simply practice the presence of God by putting aside all your distractions. If you have difficulty with this little room of the mind, bring Christ in there. Pack it full with the Word of God, meditate upon it and keep before it the immediate presence of the Lord Jesus. For the next few minutes get rid of your phone, Facebook, Twitter, Snapchat, Tinder, email and every other distraction. By practicing the presence of God and literally living moment by moment in connection with God, you can be sure to avoid the trap of carrying out natural sinful desires.

PRAYER

Heavenly Father,

In this moment, I turn my heart and my mind to You. In the next few minutes I simply want to sense what it is like to walk with You, to sit with You. Would You speak to me? Would You sit with me right now?

I love You, Father. In Jesus' name I pray. Amen.

FAST THIS WEEK

This week, take time away from media. Don't watch TV or movies. Use the internet, email, apps, your phone, any books or magazines only for necessary business rather than for entertainment. Replace your unhurried, relaxed moments with genuine rest, time with family, and time reading the Word of God and praying to Him.

WITH YOUR FAMILY

Tell your kids they will need to listen well and follow directions. They will have to walk around the house without bumping anything. Sound easy? They will also be wearing a blindfold! Blindfold your child. Without making contact, guide them around the house with your words. Now switch and allow them to guide you.

FOLLOW

- Was that easy or difficult? Why?

- Would you have been able to walk around without the voice guiding you?

- What if there were loud music playing or other voices? Would you have bumped into anything?

God wants to guide us, but we must walk in the Spirit. To know the voice of God we must block out distractions that could easily cause us to stumble.

- What is something that could be a distraction in your life?

notes

THIS WEEK'S MEMORY VERSE

"I have been crucified with Christ; it is no longer I who live, but Christ lives in me; and the life which I now live in the flesh I live by faith in the Son of God, who loved me and gave Himself for me."

Galatians 2:20

SCRIPTURE

Read Galatians 5

Focus -

"Now the works of the flesh are obvious: sexual immorality, moral impurity, promiscuity, idolatry, sorcery, hatreds, strife, jealousy, outbursts of anger, selfish ambitions, dissensions, factions, envy, drunkenness, carousing, and anything similar. I tell you about these things in advance— as I told you before—that those who practice such things will not inherit the kingdom of God."

Galatians 5:19-21

OBSERVATION

Continuing to process the idea of moving through the inner study of your heart and mind, Paul challenges us to walk by the Spirit by identifying clear expressions of sin that we all deal with in the private areas of life. These fifteen items, as they stand, may be put into four groups: sexual sins, twisted religious expressions, personal relationship struggles, and habits leading to excess. All these struggles have a tendency not only to occupy our thoughts, but each one

week one

can quickly dominate your focus and quickly pull you down. Recognize that God moves us to get rid of the sinful clutter in the private areas of life. This is accomplished through intentionally choosing the path of spiritual and physical discipline, not only to overcome these temptations and struggles, but more importantly, to walk with the Lord.

APPLICATION

The ability to overcome sin and temptation starts with focus. Today, do not try to empty your life of the sinful expressions listed by Paul in Galatians 5, but instead take time to fill your life with the presence of God, the promises found in His word, and the practice of serving Him throughout this day. See if you can come up with a specific passage of scripture for each of the four broad groups of sin listed by Paul. As a reminder, the broad categories are: sexual sin, twisted religious expressions, personal relationship struggles and sins of excess. Spend a few minutes reading through and meditating on the scriptures you have found and follow up by seeking out a brother or sister in Christ who can push you to remain faithful to the Lord.

PRAYER

Heavenly Father,

I pray that You would help me clean up my life. May the things I think about throughout this day and even the private temptations that come my way, be avoided, confessed, and restored. Thank You Lord for the amazing gift of forgiveness and help.

I love You, Father. In Jesus' name I pray. Amen.

FAST THIS WEEK

This week, take time away from media. Don't watch TV or movies. Use the internet, email, apps, your phone, any books or magazines only for necessary business rather than for entertainment. Replace your unhurried, relaxed moments with genuine rest, time with family, and time reading the Word of God and praying to Him.

WITH YOUR FAMILY

Gather some fruit from your refrigerator. Cut it up to make fruit salad. Enjoy time together at the table eating a snack and discuss these questions. First, read Galatians 5:22-23 together.

GOOD FRUIT, BAD FRUIT

- If Christ is in us, what qualities should people see in us?

- If Christ is not in us, what fruit will we produce?

- What do people say about the fruit they see in your life?

- What fruit do you see in my life?

- What fruit does the Spirit need to work in your life? How can we help?

notes

THIS WEEK'S MEMORY VERSE

"I have been crucified with Christ; it is no longer I who live, but Christ lives in me; and the life which I now live in the flesh I live by faith in the Son of God, who loved me and gave Himself for me."

Galatians 2:20

SCRIPTURE

Read Galatians 5

Focus -

"But the fruit of the Spirit is love, joy, peace, patience, kindness, goodness, faith, gentleness, self-control. Against such things there is no law. Now those who belong to Christ Jesus have crucified the flesh with its passions and desires."

Galatians 5:22-24

OBSERVATION

As you take the time to process this passage, notice that the fruit of the Spirit is a singular fruit that produces multiple results in the life of the follower of Christ. Recognize that each of the results of this singular fruit is not a list from which a believer can pick and choose. You should not think you can embrace love while ignoring self-control because that is more difficult. Or strive for peace while refusing to show kindness. The Lord is at work in your life producing a fruit that encompasses every one of these characteristics. As an explanation, because the Lord has chosen to dwell in the life of each believer, the result of that indwelling is a growth

week one

in this singular fruit of the Spirit which results in love, joy, peace, patience, kindness, goodness, faith, gentleness, and self-control.

APPLICATION

Take a few minutes and look back at your life. Can you identify an experience or a time when this fruit was growing? See if you can recognize a time when each characteristic of the Spirit's fruit was evident. What was going on the last time you were able to love? When was your last expression of real joy? What happened the last time you experienced peace. Do this for each expression of the fruit.

PRAYER

Heavenly Father,

Thank You for choosing to dwell within me. Thank You for being willing to invest Your fruit in my life. I pray that I would recognize Your presence as Your Spirit continues to grow each one of these characteristics in my life. I long to serve You Lord and I pray that my life would be pleasing to You.

I love You, Father. In Jesus' name I pray. Amen.

FAST THIS WEEK

This week, take time away from media. Don't watch TV or movies. Use the internet, email, apps, your phone, any books or magazines only for necessary business rather than for entertainment. Replace your unhurried, relaxed moments with genuine rest, time with family, and time reading the Word of God and praying to Him.

WITH YOUR FAMILY

Pick up a cake mix at the store and make it together as a family. While it is in the oven discuss these questions.

PART OF THE WHOLE

- What would happen if we left out ingredients?

- Would the cake be the same?

- Read Galatians 5:22-24.

- What are the fruit of the Spirit?

- Can we pick and choose the fruit we want? (No.)

- It is the fruit of the Spirit, singular, in your life, not fruit(s). The Holy Spirit produces one fruit in many flavors. Each flavor allows God to minister to you and through you to others in a way that meets a specific need at a specific time. What flavor do you need to experience today? What flavor do you need to share today?

- Allow the Holy Spirit to grow fruit in you. Practice memorizing the fruit of the Spirit.

notes

THIS WEEK'S MEMORY VERSE

"I have been crucified with Christ; it is no longer I who live, but Christ lives in me;.and the life which I now live in the flesh I live by faith in the Son of God, who loved me and gave Himself for me."

Galatians 2:20

SCRIPTURE

Read Galatians 5

Focus -

"But the fruit of the Spirit is love, joy, peace, patience, kindness, goodness, faith, gentleness, self-control. Against such things there is no law. Now those who belong to Christ Jesus have crucified the flesh with its passions and desires."

Galatians 5:22-24

OBSERVATION

As the focus remains on the fruit of the Spirit, notice that those who belong to Christ Jesus have crucified the flesh with its passions and desires. Crucifixion is an intentional act. No one who was ever crucified went through that experience by accident. It was deliberate. Paul reminds the believer that we must be deliberate and intentional about our faith. We must recognize that in the flesh, there is a constant struggle with our passions and desires. We have to intentionally and aggressively put away the desires of our flesh and replace those with the work of the Spirit. Each characteristic of this fruit growing in our lives comes about by discipline and in some cases, aggressive intentionality.

week one

APPLICATION

Today, choose to be intentional about growing in your faith. Are there boundaries that you need to establish? Are there relationships you need to build? Are there relationships you need to end? Because every person, regardless of background, has a curiosity with sin, there must be an aggressive intentionality about growing in faith. Rather than giving in to the temptation to see how close you can get to sin without crossing the line, become more intentional about turning your focus to growing as a believer. The key to staying in step with the Spirit of God can be found in spiritual disciplines. Map out a plan today.

PRAYER

Heavenly Father,

Help me to grow up in my faith, today. Guide me as I become more intentional in my discipline. Grow this fruit of the Spirit in my life, today.

I love You, Father. In Jesus' name I pray. Amen.

FAST THIS WEEK

This week, take time away from media. Don't watch TV or movies. Use the internet, email, apps, your phone, any books or magazines only for necessary business rather than for entertainment. Replace your unhurried, relaxed moments with genuine rest, time with family, and time reading the Word of God and praying to Him.

WITH YOUR FAMILY

Gather your family together and talk about a time they experienced the presence of God. Hand each person something like a string, bracelet, necklace, etc. Tell them this item is to remind them of the presence of God in their lives. Everytime they see this item tell them to pray and thank God for His presence.

AS YOU GO

- Have you ever felt alone?

- What did you do?

- Read John 14:27 – "Peace I leave with you; my peace I give you. I do not give to you as the world gives. Do not let your hearts be troubled and do not be afraid."

- What does this verse mean to you?

The Spirit never leaves us so we can experience His peace anytime, anywhere.

notes

THIS WEEK'S MEMORY VERSE

"I have been crucified with Christ; it is no longer I who live, but Christ lives in me; and the life which I now live in the flesh I live by faith in the Son of God, who loved me and gave Himself for me."

Galatians 2:20

SCRIPTURE

Read Galatians 5

Focus -

"But the fruit of the Spirit is love, joy, peace, patience, kindness, goodness, faith, gentleness, self-control. Against such things there is no law. Now those who belong to Christ Jesus have crucified the flesh with its passions and desires. Since we live by the Spirit, we must also follow the Spirit. We must not become conceited, provoking one another, envying one another."

Galatians 5:22-24

OBSERVATION

Paul writes, "...since we live by the Spirit, we must also follow the Spirit." During this first week of Lent, the goal is to grow. God is calling you to grow up in your faith, to learn to interact with God on a daily basis. God is calling you to follow His Spirit. This can only happen if you pay attention to where He is going. You will not be able to follow Him unless you are looking at Him. As this forty-day journey through the Lent season progresses, take this time to grow in your discipline. Take this time to genuinely follow Christ with

week one

humility, with gratitude, and with love for one another.

APPLICATION

Take time to work through the following spiritual assessment. As you evaluate your answers, do you see evidence of spiritual growth over the past 12 months? Why or Why not?

How would you rate yourself on each expression of the fruit of the Spirit? Evaluate yourself on a scale from 1 to 5. One (1) reflects "NEED TO GROW". Five (5) reflects "GREAT".

- Love
- Joy
- Peace
- Patience
- Kindness/Goodness
- Faithfulness
- Gentleness
- Self-control

PRAYER

Heavenly Father,

Help me to grow. Help me to faithfully walk with You. Speak to me about those hidden areas in my heart and mind. Guide me to live a faithful and disciplined life. Grow this fruit of the Spirit in me.

I love You, Father. In Jesus' name I pray. Amen.

FAST THIS WEEK

This week, take time away from media. Don't watch TV or movies. Use the internet, email, apps, your phone, any books or magazines only for necessary business rather than for entertainment. Replace your unhurried, relaxed moments with genuine rest, time with family, and time reading the Word of God and praying to Him.

WITH YOUR FAMILY

Grab 5-10 random objects from around your home and arrange them on the table. Bring your kids in and let them look at them for a minute. Then have them close their eyes and change five things. Ask them to open their eyes and identify the five changes. Try this as many times as you would like or let them change things for you.

TAKING INVENTORY

- Was it difficult to find the changes?
- Why were you able to find the changes? (Because you studied the original.)
- Read 2 Corinthians 5:17. Why should we want to change?

In your life, you can take notice of things that need to change. Thankfully, when Christ is Lord of our life, the Holy Spirit works on the fruit in our lives, but we must be willing.

notes

week two

THE DINING ROOM

From the study we went into the dining room, the room of appetites and desires. I spent a lot of time and hard work here trying to satisfy my wants. I said to Him, "This is a favorite room. I am quite sure You will be pleased with what we serve."

He seated Himself at the table with me and asked, "What is on the menu for dinner?" "Well," I said, "my favorite dishes: money, academic degrees and stocks, with newspaper articles of fame and fortune as side dishes." These were the things I liked—secular fare. When the food was placed before Him, He said nothing, but I observed that He did not eat it. I said to Him, "Master, don't You care for this food? What is the trouble?"

He answered, "I have food to eat that you do not know of. If you want food that really satisfies you, do the will of the Father. Stop seeking your own pleasures, desires, and satisfaction. Seek to please Him. That food will satisfy you."

There at the table He gave me a taste of the joy of doing God's will. What flavor! There is no food like it in the world. It alone satisfies.

THE LIVING ROOM

From the dining room we walked into the living room. This room was intimate and comfortable. I liked it. It had a fireplace, overstuffed chairs, sofa, and a quiet atmosphere. He said, "This is indeed a delightful room. Let us come here often. It is secluded and quiet, and we can fellowship together."

Well, as a young Christian I was thrilled. I couldn't think of anything I would rather do than have a few minutes with Christ in close companionship. He promised, "I will be here early every morning. Meet Me here, and we will start the day together."

So morning after morning, I would come downstairs to the living room. He would take a book of the Bible from the case. We would open it and read it together. He would unfold to me the wonder of God's saving truths. My heart sang as He shared the love and grace He had toward me. These were wonderful times.

However, little by little, under the pressure of many responsibilities, this time began to be shortened. Why, I'm not sure. I thought I was too busy to spend regular time with Christ. This was not intentional, you understand. It just happened that way. Finally, not only was the time shortened, but I began to miss days now and then. Urgent matters would crowd out the quiet times of conversation with Jesus.

I remember one morning rushing downstairs, eager to be on my way. I passed the living room and noticed that the door was opened. Looking in, I saw a fire in the fireplace and Jesus was sitting there. Suddenly in dismay I thought to myself, "He is my guest. I invited Him into my heart! He has come as my Savior and Friend, and yet I am neglecting Him."

I stopped, turned and hesitantly went in. With downcast glance, I said, "Master, forgive me. Have You been here all these mornings?" "Yes," He said, "I told you I would be here every morning to meet with you. Remember, I love you. I have redeemed you at a great cost. I value your friendship. Even if you cannot keep the quiet time for your own sake, do it for Mine."

The truth that Christ desires my companionship, that He

wants me to be with Him and waits for me, has done more to transform my quiet time with God than any other single fact. Don't let Christ wait alone in the living room of your heart, but every day find time when, with your Bible and in prayer, you may be together with Him.

FAST THIS WEEK

What will you remove this week from "the Dining Room and Living Room" of your life so that you might better focus your heart and mind on God?

This week, fast in two parts. First, select one 24 hour period where you choose not to eat or drink anything but water. Use your regular meal times to memorize Scripture, read the Word, pray, and write in a journal your questions, concerns, and thoughts about Lent and the things you hear God saying to you.

For the second part, fast from sleep one hour each day. Set your clock to wake up one hour early. With Bible, pen, and paper go to a comfortable place. Write out your schedule for the day and pray through all you have to do. Write the names of people you know you will see that day. Pray for them. Write the names of people you haven't seen in awhile. Pray for them and make a plan to contact them later that day. Use the time to read and memorize Scripture.

you are what you eat

THIS WEEK'S MEMORY VERSE

*"And Jesus answered and said to her,
"Martha, Martha, you are worried and troubled
about many things. But one thing is needed,
and Mary has chosen that good part, which
will not be taken away from her."*

Luke 10:41-42

SCRIPTURE

Read Daniel 1

Focus -

*"But Daniel purposed in his heart that he would not defile
himself with the portion of the king's delicacies, nor with
the wine which he drank..."*

Daniel 1:8

OBSERVATION

The words of the doctor were frank and forceful. "You are what you eat", he said. "If you would change your blood sugar, your blood pressure, and the level of pain in your knees, you must change your eating habits."

Although these are fictitious words, similar words are spoken most every day by doctors in the U. S. Similar words could be spoken by the ONE examining our spiritual eating habits. Daniel determined to eat only that which would help him be physically and mentally strong. He and his friends proved (in just 10 days) the benefit proper food has on our bodies (see Daniel 1:15).

What would the Great Physician say about your spiritual eating habits? In the Dining Room of your heart, would He

week two

find a growing appetite for God's Word, or would He see the discarded garbage of spiritual junk food?

APPLICATION

Just like we control our food intake, we also control our spiritual appetite. We can develop a greater hunger for God's Word. Will you take a step of faith today in that important direction? Will you increase your spiritual appetite?

PRAYER

Heavenly Father,

Thank You for giving me Your Word. I confess with Jeremiah (15:16), "Your words were found, and I ate them, and Your word was to me the joy and rejoicing of my heart; For I am called by Your name, O Lord God of hosts."

I love You, Father. In Jesus' name I pray. Amen.

 ## FAST THIS WEEK

This week, fast in two parts. First, select one 24 hour period where you choose not to eat or drink anything but water. Use your regular meal times to memorize Scripture, read the Word, pray, and write in a journal your questions, concerns, and thoughts about Lent and the things you hear God saying to you.

For the second part, fast from sleep one hour each day. Set your clock to wake up one hour early. With Bible, pen, and paper go to a comfortable place. Write out your schedule for the day and pray through all you have to do. Write the names of people you know you will see that day. Pray for them. Write the names of people you haven't seen in awhile. Pray for them and make a plan to contact them later that day. Use the time to read and memorize Scripture.

WITH YOUR FAMILY

As a family, choose a favorite type of food. Google creative ways to take your choice and prepre that food in a new way. Make your shopping list, purchase ingredients, and prepare the meal together. Everyone has a job whether it is in the actual meal preparation or decorating the table. The goal is to work together right down to cleaning up the dishes.

DISH DELISH

- What are some good and bad foods we put in our bodies?

- What is the difference between spiritual food and the food we ate tonight?

- Why do we not like to eat baby food?

- Why is it important to only give God our best? Is it similar to being on our best behavior when guests come over?

notes

THIS WEEK'S MEMORY VERSE

"And Jesus answered and said to her, "Martha, Martha, you are worried and troubled about many things. But one thing is needed, and Mary has chosen that good part, which will not be taken away from her."

Luke 10:41-42

SCRIPTURE

Read Hebrews 5

Focus -

"For everyone who partakes only of milk is unskilled in the word of righteousness, for he is a babe. But solid food belongs to those who are of full age, that is, those who by reason of use have their senses exercised to discern both good and evil."

Hebrews 5:13 - 14

OBSERVATION

What differences exist between babies and adults? Aside from the obvious (size and speech) one major difference is the ability to clean and feed one's self. The same is true spiritually. Spiritual babes require soft food and someone to feed them, while adults feed themselves and enjoy solid food.

The writer of Hebrews told his readers they were spiritual babes requiring milk. What would the Lord say to you as He examines the dining room of your heart? Do you enjoy the daily nourishment of God's Word, or are you waiting for others to feed you?

week two

APPLICATION

You are responsible for the dining room of your life and its bill of fare. You can survive on baby food, or you can thrive on the meat of God's Word. Will you pray to become one who is skilled in the Word of righteousness?

PRAYER

Heavenly Father,

Thank You for the people who have lovingly fed me spiritually. I have known You long enough to be more mature than I am presently. You've said that I should not live on bread alone, but on every Word proceeding from Your mouth. Please forgive my lack of diligence in reading and studying Your Word, and please feed me today.

I love You, Father. In Jesus' name I pray. Amen.

FAST THIS WEEK

This week, fast in two parts. First, select one 24 hour period where you choose not to eat or drink anything but water. Use your regular meal times to memorize Scripture, read the Word, pray, and write in a journal your questions, concerns, and thoughts about Lent and the things you hear God saying to you.

For the second part, fast from sleep one hour each day. Set your clock to wake up one hour early. With Bible, pen, and paper go to a comfortable place. Write out your schedule for the day and pray through all you have to do. Write the names of people you know you will see that day. Pray for them. Write the names of people you haven't seen in awhile. Pray for them and make a plan to contact them later that day. Use the time to read and memorize Scripture.

WITH YOUR FAMILY

Push back the furniture, unplug the TV, and plan a camp out. You could put up a tent or make a tent by draping sheets over chairs. Cover your floor with a sheet or blanket and have a picnic. Turn out the lights and use flashlights to make shadows on the wall or ceiling. Use a lantern to tell stories in the dark. Whatever you do, have fun, and make a memory.

OPERATION LIVING ROOM CAMPOUT

- What's your favorite thing about the place where we live?

- What makes a house a home?

- Do you remember what it was like to be a baby?

- What can you do that a baby can't do?

- What do you look forward to doing as an adult that you can't do right now because you are still too young?

notes

THIS WEEK'S MEMORY VERSE

"And Jesus answered and said to her, "Martha, Martha, you are worried and troubled about many things. But one thing is needed, and Mary has chosen that good part, which will not be taken away from her."

Luke 10:41-42

SCRIPTURE

Read Isaiah 55

Focus -

"Why do you spend your money for what is not bread, and your wages for what does not satisfy? Listen carefully to Me, and eat what is good, and let your soul delight itself in abundance."

Isaiah 55:2 - 3

OBSERVATION

Mick Jagger has made a boatload of money singing the phrase, "I can't get no satisfaction." Although his grammar wasn't the best, he did serve a good purpose in making us think about our "satisfaction ratio." More important than your credit rating is the ratio of inner peace and satisfaction corresponding to the investments you make for it in time and money.

If you invest time and money wisely in eternal things (people and God's Word) you will also enjoy inner peace and satisfaction. If, however, the living room of your heart reveals a treasure trove of temporal values then you are "singing along with Mick". We're just not wired to be satisfied with money and things. Your inner thirst testifies to the truth of Isaiah's words.

week two

APPLICATION

If my heart is in the wrong place, I can do something about it, for where my treasure is, there will my heart be also (Matthew 6:21).

PRAYER

Heavenly Father,

Deep in my heart I know the most important things in life are not things. I long for priorities that reflect eternal values rather than temporary pleasures. Please, show me how much and where to give my money, which is really Your money on loan to me.

I love You, Father. In Jesus' name I pray. Amen.

FAST THIS WEEK

This week, fast in two parts. First, select one 24 hour period where you choose not to eat or drink anything but water. Use your regular meal times to memorize Scripture, read the Word, pray, and write in a journal your questions, concerns, and thoughts about Lent and the things you hear God saying to you.

For the second part, fast from sleep one hour each day. Set your clock to wake up one hour early. With Bible, pen, and paper go to a comfortable place. Write out your schedule for the day and pray through all you have to do. Write the names of people you know you will see that day. Pray for them. Write the names of people you haven't seen in awhile. Pray for them and make a plan to contact them later that day. Use the time to read and memorize Scripture.

WITH YOUR FAMILY

Invite a family over to eat appetizers and play Family Feud. You can either purchase this game or watch an episode on YouTube for instructions on how to play. Google "Family Feud" to find questions and answers. The family who loses provides ice cream.

LIVING ROOM GAME NIGHT

- What worries you?

- How can relying on one another help calm those worries?

- What can you pray to help you overcome your worries?

- Does your family have a need you can ask God's help with? Pray about that need as a family.

- How can you pray for the family you invited over for games?

notes

THIS WEEK'S MEMORY VERSE

"And Jesus answered and said to her, "Martha, Martha, you are worried and troubled about many things. But one thing is needed, and Mary has chosen that good part, which will not be taken away from her."

Luke 10:41-42

SCRIPTURE

Read Luke 10

Focus -

"...and a certain woman named Martha welcomed Him into her house. And she had a sister called Mary, who also sat at Jesus' feet and heard His word. But Martha was distracted with much serving, and she approached Him and said, "Lord, do you not care that my sister has left me to serve alone? Therefore tell her to help me." And Jesus answered and said to her, "Martha, Martha, you are worried and troubled about many things. But one thing is needed, and Mary has chosen that good part, which will not be taken away from her."

Isaiah 55:2 - 3

OBSERVATION

The good is always the enemy of the best. Missing the best is never worth all the other good things, and the good things can be really good. Actively serving the Lord is a really good thing. Martha was a good servant and she was so pleased to have the Lord Jesus in her home for a meal. You probably would be, also.

As she busily served Him, she noticed her younger sister

week two

Mary wasn't, and it really bothered her. The question she posed to Jesus revealed her heart. "Lord, do You not care…?"

Stop right there!

Her frantic service blinded her to the most basic of truths, that there could ever be a situation where the Lord would not care about her. How about you? Are you like Martha? Are you busy in so many good things you don't have time to sit at Jesus' feet in the living room of your life and hear His Word?

If so, you're too busy. For all of us "one thing is needed," which provides the energy to keep our service in proper perspective.

APPLICATION

You will not find time to sit at Jesus' feet and hear His word. You must make time for it. Would you be willing to turn off the TV earlier tonight and go to bed earlier, all for the purpose of getting up earlier to spend focused, unhurried time with the Lord Jesus? The precious things you'll hear will never be taken away from you.

PRAYER

Heavenly Father,

Please forgive me for being too busy for You. I realize that time alone with You is the one great need in my life, and by Your grace I will make the changes I need to make that happen. I want the BEST! Thank You, Lord!

I love You, Father. In Jesus' name I pray. Amen.

FAST THIS WEEK

This week, fast in two parts. First, select one 24 hour period where you choose not to eat or drink anything but water. Use your regular meal times to memorize Scripture, read the Word, pray, and write in a journal your questions, concerns, and thoughts about Lent and the things you hear God saying to you.

For the second part, fast from sleep one hour each day. Set your clock to wake up one hour early. With Bible, pen, and paper go to a comfortable place. Write out your schedule for the day and pray through all you have to do. Write the names of people you know you will see that day. Pray for them. Write the names of people you haven't seen in awhile. Pray for them and make a plan to contact them later that day. Use the time to read and memorize Scripture.

WITH YOUR FAMILY

Choose a movie to watch as a family that has a strong good verses evil theme, for example: Snow White, Beauty and The Beast, or Hercules. Pop some corn and invite another family over. After viewing the movie, talk about the good/evil roles in the movie.

FAMILY NIGHT AT THE MOVIES

God created everything and said it was good, but sin corrupte the world and everything in it.

- Why is it important to look for the good in our lives?

- Why should we be on guard for the bad?

- Why is it important to be a good example?

notes

THIS WEEK'S MEMORY VERSE

"And Jesus answered and said to her,
"Martha, Martha, you are worried and troubled
about many things. But one thing is needed,
and Mary has chosen that good part, which
will not be taken away from her."

Luke 10:41-42

SCRIPTURE

Read Luke 15

Focus -

"Then all the tax collectors and the sinners drew near
to Him to hear Him. And the Pharisees and scribes
complained, saying, "This Man receives sinners and eats
with them."

Luke 15:1 - 2

OBSERVATION

Eating alone isn't much fun. The savor of the food is nice, but isn't much of a companion. Consequently, we often seek company for meals, and the company we seek is a reflection of our heart. That's the problem the religious professionals had with Jesus' meals. He chose company from the "bottom feeders" of society. Actually, they chose Him, too, for they found in Him reception and respect rather than the condemnation they felt from so many others. When the Pharisees and scribes said, "This Man receives sinners and eats with them" they weren't offering a compliment. Rather, they were hurling an insult. They were indicting Him for not knowing the character of those He took to lunch.

Their blind hearts had no room for compassion, so their

week two

dinner table had no room for known sinners. I find this to be one of the most difficult of the traits of Jesus to emulate. It's just easier to eat with Christian friends all the time than to make room for unbelievers.

APPLICATION

As Christ enters the dining room of your heart does He find you sharing meals with lost people and conversing with them, or are you content to eat alone or with only the righteous? Let's give this important area of our life to our Savior, the One to whom sinners drew near.

PRAYER

Heavenly Father,

Thank You for receiving me when I was a sinner, and how well I know I still am! Please forgive my Pharisaical attitude, and replace it with a heart of love and compassion for sinners…sinners like me.

I love You, Father. In Jesus' name I pray. Amen.

FAST THIS WEEK

This week, fast in two parts. First, select one 24 hour period where you choose not to eat or drink anything but water. Use your regular meal times to memorize Scripture, read the Word, pray, and write in a journal your questions, concerns, and thoughts about Lent and the things you hear God saying to you.

For the second part, fast from sleep one hour each day. Set your clock to wake up one hour early. With Bible, pen, and paper go to a comfortable place. Write out your schedule for the day and pray through all you have to do. Write the names of people you know you will see that day. Pray for them. Write the names of people you haven't seen in awhile. Pray for them and make a plan to contact them later that day. Use the time to read and memorize Scripture.

WITH YOUR FAMILY

Turn down the lights and get a flashlight. Take turns creating shadow puppets on the living room wall.

SHADOW PUPPETS

Talk about how the moon reflects the sun like a mirror and how we should reflect, and represent God's Son.

- How can we be a great reflection of Jesus this week?

- Who can we talk with this week about the love of Jesus? Who needs to see God's reflection in us?

- What can we do as family this week to minister to a neighbor, shut-in, or new family in our community?

notes

week three

THE WORK ROOM

Before long, He asked, "Do you have a work room in your home?" Out in the garage of the home of my heart I had a workbench and some equipment, but I was not doing much with it. Once in a while I would play around with a few little gadgets, but I wasn't producing anything substantial.

I led Him out there. He looked over the workbench and said, "Well, this is quite well furnished. What are you producing with your life for the Kingdom of God?" He looked at one or two little toys that I had thrown together on a bench and held one up to me. "Is this the sort of thing you are doing for others in your Christian life?" "Well," I said, "Lord, I know it isn't much, and I really want to do more, but after all, I don't seem to have strength or skill to do more."

"Would you like to do better?" He asked. "Certainly," I replied. "All right. Let me have your hands. Now relax in Me and let My Spirit work through you. I know that you are unskilled, clumsy, and awkward, but the Holy Spirit is the Master Workman, and if He controls your hands and your heart, He will work through you." Stepping around behind me and putting His strong hands under mine, He held the tools in His skilled fingers and began to work through me. The more I relaxed and trusted Him, the more He was able to do with my life.

FAST THIS WEEK

What will you remove this week from the work room of your life so that you might better focus your heart and mind on God?

Consider the work you do, your job, your career, your family, and your volunteer service. You may have a "TO DO" list, a list of things you have to get done that day or week in order to be successful in your job. Today, create a "STOP DOING" list. Prayerfully consider those actions or activities that appear necessary to your job, but actually distract you from the work that adds real value to you and those around you. Select several things from your "STOP DOING" list to put into practice this week.

Fast from overwork. Work is important. God has called you to it. But in our culture we easily give in to the temptation to spend too much effort or energy trying to amass a greater fortune, often to the detriment of our families. This week, go home for lunch. Go home early. Refuse to take work home. If your work is in the home, set a time to "stop work" and invest that unhurried time with your family.

THIS WEEK'S MEMORY VERSE

"My Father is glorified by this: that you produce much fruit and prove to be My disciples."

John 15:8

SCRIPTURE

Read Psalm 139

Focus -

"For it was You who created my inward parts; You knit me together in my mother's womb. I will praise You because I have been remarkably and wonderfully made. Your works are wonderful, and I know this very well. My bones were not hidden from You when I was made in secret, when I was formed in the depths of the earth."

Psalm 139:13 - 15

OBSERVATION

The author of this passage is quick to confess that he recognizes that God made him and how valuable he is to God. The passage specifically points out how God thinks of him and how valuable he is to God.

APPLICATION

Have you ever felt like you had no value? Maybe at times you think too much about your faults. Allow this passage to remind you of what God thinks of you, which is VALUABLE. Your self-worth should be based on what God thinks, nothing else.

week three

PRAYER

Heavenly Father,

Thank You for creating me. Forgive me when I focus on my faults more than what You think about me. Thank You for reminding me through this passage of how valuable I am and how I belong to You.

I love You, Father. In Jesus' name I pray. Amen.

 FAST THIS WEEK

Consider the work you do, your job, your career, your family, and your volunteer service. You may have a "TO DO" list, a list of things you have to get done that day or week in order to be successful in your job. Today, create a "STOP DOING" list. Prayerfully consider those actions or activities that appear necessary to your job, but actually distract you from the work that adds real value to you and those around you. Select several things from your "STOP DOING" list to put into practice this week.

Fast from overwork. Work is important. God has called you to it. But in our culture we easily give in to the temptation to spend too much effort or energy trying to amass a greater fortune, often to the detriment of our families. This week, go home for lunch. Go home early. Refuse to take work home. If your work is in the home, set a time to "stop work" and invest that unhurried time with your family.

WITH YOUR FAMILY

Get together and clean the garage as a family. Play music, work together, and create simple tasks in order to make this as fun as possible. Once finished, gather on your driveway, if it is warm enough, and eat a snack while taking in the work you have done.

THE GREAT GARAGE CLEANUP

- How does our family use the garage? (storage, park cars, work space, etc).

- For a lot of people, the garage is a place where work gets done. For example, a lot of people keep tools in the garage. This week we are going to talk about the work we do and the work God wants us to do. What work do you do during the week? (school, job, sports, chores, etc)

- Did you know that God wants to work through you to do great things for him? He could use anything He wants, yet He wants to let you in on the work He is doing.

- How can you allow God to use you to do His work? (Trust Him, obey Him, talk to others about Him, don't get so busy that you don't have time for Him, etc.)

- Pray for each other, for ways that God can use you to do His work this week.

notes

THIS WEEK'S MEMORY VERSE

"My Father is glorified by this: that you produce much fruit and prove to be My disciples."

John 15:8

SCRIPTURE

Read Exodus 4

Focus -

"But Moses replied to the Lord, 'Please, Lord, I have never been eloquent, either in the past or recently or since You have been speaking to Your servant, because I am slow and hesitant in speech.' Yahweh said to him, 'Who made the human mouth? Who makes him mute or deaf, seeing or blind? Is it not I, Yahweh?'"

Exodus 4:10 - 11

OBSERVATION

Moses, shared a reason for why he thought God couldn't use him. He thought he wasn't qualified to be used by God due to a speech problem that he apparently had. Moses didn't think his speech was good enough.

APPLICATION

Have you ever reacted the way Moses did in the scripture? Have you ever thought of a reason why you couldn't be used by God? Maybe you don't feel adequate. Perhaps you believe you're not qualified to serve because you don't have a specific talent or supernatural gift. But that's not true. God has given you everything you need for life and godliness. He has called you to be salt and light in your world and given

week three

you everything you need to accomplish whatever He's set before you.

PRAYER

Heavenly Father,

Thanks for providing specific talents and gifts to me so I can be used by You. Even though there are times I don't feel adequate, I trust You. I trust You to use me here on earth. I'm grateful that You used Moses and his experience in the scripture to teach me that You can use me and the talents with which You've blessed me.

I love You, Father. In Jesus' name I pray. Amen.

FAST THIS WEEK

Consider the work you do, your job, your career, your family, and your volunteer service. You may have a "TO DO" list, a list of things you have to get done that day or week in order to be successful in your job. Today, create a "STOP DOING" list. Prayerfully consider those actions or activities that appear necessary to your job, but actually distract you from the work that adds real value to you and those around you. Select several things from your "STOP DOING" list to put into practice this week.

Fast from overwork. Work is important. God has called you to it. But in our culture we easily give in to the temptation to spend too much effort or energy trying to amass a greater fortune, often to the detriment of our families. This week, go home for lunch. Go home early. Refuse to take work home. If your work is in the home, set a time to "stop work" and invest that unhurried time with your family.

 ## WITH YOUR FAMILY

Grab some items from your house that perish quickly (such as fruit or some other food item), some items that might take a long time to perish (for example, scissors, a rock, etc.), and items that represent activities your kids are involved in (basketball, pencil, or backpack to represent school work, etc.) With your family consider these questions.

THINGS THAT FADE

- Ask, "Will this ever fade away?", as you hold up each item. You might need to help explain that homework is important but it will eventually fade away. Even a brick or rock will corrode and fade away eventually, etc. The idea is for them to understand that EVERYTHING will fade away, except for the work we do for God.

- What are works that God can do through us that won't fade away? (Telling people about Christ, encouraging others, etc.)

- We have to work hard for things that will fade away. For example, food fades away but we have to work for it to survive. However, we must make time in our lives to allow God to work through us to impact others in ways that can never fade away. How can we do that?

notes

THIS WEEK'S MEMORY VERSE

"My Father is glorified by this: that you produce much fruit and prove to be My disciples."

John 15:8

SCRIPTURE

Read 1 Peter 4

Focus -

"Based on the gift each one has received, use it to serve others, as good managers of the varied grace of God."

1 Peter 4:10

OBSERVATION

In this passage, the author encourages you to serve others with the gifts God has given you. God has blessed you with specific gifts He intends you to use often.

APPLICATION

Are you aware of the gifts God has given you? Take time to recognize and list your specific gifts and use them in the lives of others. Not everyone has the same gifts. Thank God for the gifts He's given you and ask Him to enable you to use them for His glory.

PRAYER

Heavenly Father,

Thank You for blessing me with specific gifts. Forgive me when I don't use them as I should. Forgive me when I misuse

week three

them. I choose to be used by You and to use the gifts You've given me.

I love You, Father. In Jesus' name I pray. Amen.

 FAST THIS WEEK

Consider the work you do, your job, your career, your family, and your volunteer service. You may have a "TO DO" list, a list of things you have to get done that day or week in order to be successful in your job. Today, create a "STOP DOING" list. Prayerfully consider those actions or activities that appear necessary to your job, but actually distract you from the work that adds real value to you and those around you. Select several things from your "STOP DOING" list to put into practice this week.

Fast from overwork. Work is important. God has called you to it. But in our culture we easily give in to the temptation to spend too much effort or energy trying to amass a greater fortune, often to the detriment of our families. This week, go home for lunch. Go home early. Refuse to take work home. If your work is in the home, set a time to "stop work" and invest that unhurried time with your family.

WITH YOUR FAMILY

Grab a few items you can wrap and give to your family members (keep in mind the items can be really simple, like a candy bar). Gather your family together and tell them that you have gifts for each of them. Hand them their gifts and tell them they need to wait until the devotional is over to open it.

WHAT'S YOUR GIFT?

- Why did I give you a gift? (Because you love us.)

- Did you do anything to earn those gifts? (No.)

- What kind of gifts has God given us? This is a great time to talk about the gift of Salvation, the most important gift God gives. We did nothing to deserve it. Take time to discover if everyone in the family has placed their faith in Christ. Share your own testimony about the day God gave you the gift of Salvation.

- What other gifts has God given us? (Spiritual gifts)

- How can we use the gifts God has given us to bring glory to Him while we are here on this earth?

- Take a moment to go around and share specific gifts you believe God has given members of your family. This is a great time to encourage each other. Pray and ask God to help you encourage one another to use your gifts for His glory.

notes

THIS WEEK'S MEMORY VERSE

"My Father is glorified by this: that you produce much fruit and prove to be My disciples."

John 15:8

SCRIPTURE

Read John 15

Focus -

"My Father is glorified by this: that you produce much fruit and prove to be My disciples."

John 15:8

OBSERVATION

The Apostle John informs us that when you produce spiritual fruit, it brings glory to God, Your Father, and proves that you belong to God.

APPLICATION

What keeps you from producing spiritual fruit? Laziness? Apathy? Business? God intends for you to produce fruit as you work for Him while on earth. Choose to produce fruit as you live out your faith each and every day. The fruit you bear will bring glory to God and point people to His Son, Jesus Christ.

PRAYER

Heavenly Father,

I choose to produce fruit, to be useful for You, and to point people to Your Son, Jesus Christ. Forgive me. I desire to

week three

get rid of the things that keep me from producing fruit. I'm honored to bring glory to You by producing fruit.

I love You, Father. In Jesus' name I pray. Amen.

FAST THIS WEEK

Consider the work you do, your job, your career, your family, and your volunteer service. You may have a "TO DO" list, a list of things you have to get done that day or week in order to be successful in your job. Today, create a "STOP DOING" list. Prayerfully consider those actions or activities that appear necessary to your job, but actually distract you from the work that adds real value to you and those around you. Select several things from your "STOP DOING" list to put into practice this week.

Fast from overwork. Work is important. God has called you to it. But in our culture we easily give in to the temptation to spend too much effort or energy trying to amass a greater fortune, often to the detriment of our families. This week, go home for lunch. Go home early. Refuse to take work home. If your work is in the home, set a time to "stop work" and invest that unhurried time with your family.

WITH YOUR FAMILY

Give each member of your family a piece of paper. Have them go to a place where there is a mirror and draw a picture of themselves. If they can write, have them write down words that they or others have used to describe them. (If they can't write, have them share out loud.) Come back together to share your pictures with each other.

THE GREATEST TREASURE

- How would you describe yourself?

- How have others described you?

- Has anyone ever said anything hurtful about how you look or who you are?

- How do you think God would describe you?

- This is a great moment to read Psalm 139 as a family. Have your family point out key phrases that the passage uses to describe how God made you.

- Did you know that God not only made you the way you are, but He wants to work through you to change people's lives?

- Pray as a family about ways that you can push aside insecurities and trust God and allow Him to work through you.

notes

THIS WEEK'S MEMORY VERSE

"My Father is glorified by this: that you produce much fruit and prove to be My disciples."

John 15:8

SCRIPTURE

Read John 14

Focus -

"And I will ask the Father, and He will give you another advocate to help you and be with you forever."

John 14:16

OBSERVATION

The Apostle John shares with us that God has provided you with an advocate, the Holy Spirit, in times of need. He expresses that the Holy Spirit will always be available to help us. We're not limited to His help when we're in need. He helps us all the time.

APPLICATION

When God calls on you to serve Him and work for Him, do you need help? When you do, God provides a helper, the Holy Spirit. When we work for God you will need strength, wisdom, discernment, and direction. Trust in and rely on His help.

PRAYER

Heavenly Father,

Thank You for providing a helper as I work for You. I

week three

recognize that I can't work for You alone. I choose to rely on the Holy Spirit for help.

I love You, Father. In Jesus' name I pray. Amen.

FAST THIS WEEK

Consider the work you do, your job, your career, your family, and your volunteer service. You may have a "TO DO" list, a list of things you have to get done that day or week in order to be successful in your job. Today, create a "STOP DOING" list. Prayerfully consider those actions or activities that appear necessary to your job, but actually distract you from the work that adds real value to you and those around you. Select several things from your "STOP DOING" list to put into practice this week.

Fast from overwork. Work is important. God has called you to it. But in our culture we easily give in to the temptation to spend too much effort or energy trying to amass a greater fortune, often to the detriment of our families. This week, go home for lunch. Go home early. Refuse to take work home. If your work is in the home, set a time to "stop work" and invest that unhurried time with your family.

WITH YOUR FAMILY

Grab some items from your house with which you can make a tower (blocks, marshmallows, Legos, books, etc.). Gather your family and tell them that they are going to build a tower. Have each family member build a tower, one at a time, and only give them 30 seconds to do so. However, assign each family member a different "challenge" they have to overcome. For example:

- One must build a tower while wearing a blindfold.
- One must build a tower but they cannot use their hands.
- Two people must build a tower together but cannot speak.

The idea is to face challenges building the tower. Have them build the tower again, but this time give them a helper. Have each family member go through the activity with the same challenges. Only this time, allow them to have a partner who helps them. The partner is not limited by the challenges.

TRICKY TOWER

- Was it easier to build the tower when you were by yourself or when you had a helper?

- Why was it easier with a helper?

- What are some things God might ask us to do that are hard?

- Does God expect us to do it alone? Or does He give us help? (He gives us help from other people, but the Holy Spirit never leaves)

God doesn't just give us tasks and leave us all alone to accomplish them. He helps us through His Holy Spirit in our lives.

notes

_____

_____

_____

_____

_____

_____

_____

_____

_____

_____

_____

_____

_____

_____

_____

_____

_____

week four

week four

THE REC ROOM

He asked me if I had a rec room where I went for fun and fellowship. I was hoping He would not ask about that. There were certain associations and activities that I wanted to keep for myself.

One evening when I was on my way out with some buddies, He stopped me with a glance and asked, "Are you going out?" I replied, "Yes." "Good," He said, "I would like to go with you." "Oh," I answered rather awkwardly." "I don't think, Lord Jesus, that you would really enjoy where we are going. Let's go out together tomorrow night. Tomorrow night we will go to a Bible class at church, but tonight I have another appointment."

"I am sorry," He said. "I thought that when I came into your home, we were going to do everything together, to be close companions. I just want you to know that I am willing to go with you." "Well," I mumbled, slipping out the door, "we will go someplace together tomorrow night."

That evening I spent some miserable hours. I felt rotten. What kind of friend was I to Jesus, deliberately leaving Him out of my life, doing things and going places that I knew very well He would not enjoy?

When I returned that evening, there was a light in His room, and I went up to talk it over with Him. I said "Lord, I have learned my lesson. I know now that I can't have a good time without You. From now on, we will do everything together." Then we went down into the rec room of the house. He transformed it. He brought new friends, new excitement, and new joys. Laughter and music have been ringing through the house ever since.

FAST THIS WEEK

What will you remove this week from the rec room of your life so that you might better focus your heart and mind on God?

We live in a world filled with extracurricular activities. Sports, band, clubs, professional organizations, and opportunities abound for us to fill our time with superfluous activity that doesn't add real value to you or anyone else. Evaluate your recreational activities. Do sports, band, or other forms of entertainment distract you from serving others or worshiping God? Each day this week, set aside a leisure activity. Use the time to be with family, volunteer in your community, or spend unhurried time in Scripture.

For those activities that seem necessary, like sports practices, band rehearsals, etc., make a list of the people who will participate with you. Pray for them each day and look for ways to encourage them to experience life in Christ.

THIS WEEK'S MEMORY VERSE

""Do not let any unwholesome talk come out of your mouths, but only what is helpful for building others up according to their needs, that it may benefit those who listen. And do not grieve the Holy Spirit of God, with whom you were sealed for the day of redemption."

Ephesians 4:29 - 30

SCRIPTURE

Read 1 Corinthians 15

Focus -

"Do not be misled: "Bad company corrupts good character." Come back to your senses as you ought, and stop sinning."

1 Corinthians 15:33 - 34

OBSERVATION

In this passage we certainly see the truth that if we hang with the wrong people, our character suffers. Building a strong testimony takes a lifetime, but we can lose it in the second of a bad choice. Our friends define us. They share and help shape our likes and dislikes, our passions and fears, our sins, and hopefully spiritual joys. They can encourage us or bring us down. They can speak truth into our lives or help us justify wrong choices. We must choose wisely and with great care who walks this path with us.

APPLICATION

I know what you are thinking. Yup, I have some bad friendships. What should I do? How can I be a witness and

week four

not just cut them off? While it is never easy to begin to walk out of the woods, simply stand on truth. Choose Jesus. Once you decide to "do what's right", the Lord will begin to help you be a friend that says, "No, that's wrong" and a friend that says, "Come with me." You will be amazed at the freedom of choosing Jesus and doing right. Once you have made up your mind, the circumstances and situations that follow in the coming days will be filled with joy because the Lord is with you, not being pushed away by you. Choose Jesus.

PRAYER

Heavenly Father,

Help me to choose Jesus. Help me to be a great friend. Please surround me with people that desire to glorify You and be a blessing to others as we walk this wonderful path of life together. You are so gracious and loving. You have given us the blessing of knowing You. May we give You all of ourselves that we may be used purposefully by You all the days of our lives.

I love You, Father. In Jesus' name I pray. Amen.

FAST THIS WEEK

What will you remove this week from the rec room of your life so that you might better focus your heart and mind on God?

We live in a world filled with extracurricular activities. Sports, band, clubs, professional organizations, and opportunities abound for us to fill our time with superfluous activity that doesn't add real value to you or anyone else. Evaluate your recreational activities. Do sports, band, or other forms of entertainment distract you from serving others or worshiping God? Each day this week, set aside a leisure activity. Use the time to be with family, volunteer in your community, or spend unhurried time in Scripture.

For those activities that seem necessary, like sports practices, band rehearsals, etc., make a list of the people who will participate with you. Pray for them each day and look for ways to encourage them to experience life in Christ.

WITH YOUR FAMILY

Today you will talk to your kids about choosing good friends. Grab two pieces of paper and some jelly. Place jelly on one piece of paper. Keep the other paper clean. Ask, "What will happen if we rub the two pages together? "

CHOOSE WISELY

- Who could the clean piece of paper represent?

- Who represents the paper with the jelly on it?

- What will bad company or friends do to us? (Show me your friends, I'll show you your future.)

- How can we love others without allowing being negatively influenced by them?

- Think about your friends. How do they influence you? How are they rubbing off on you?

notes

THIS WEEK'S MEMORY VERSE

""Do not let any unwholesome talk come out of your mouths, but only what is helpful for building others up according to their needs, that it may benefit those who listen. And do not grieve the Holy Spirit of God, with whom you were sealed for the day of redemption."

Ephesians 4:29 - 30

SCRIPTURE

Read Matthew 6

Focus -

"No one can serve two masters. Either you will hate the one and love the other, or you will be devoted to the one and despise the other."

Matthew 6:24

OBSERVATION

Treading the line can be very dangerous. It shows we can't make a solid decision. One minute we are for truth and then in the next moment we are for sin. After awhile we become bitter towards the conviction and bound by the sin. When we go back and forth from truth to sin, we are serving two very different masters. One, the Heavenly One, wants to bless us with love, joy, and peace. The other wants to bind us and ultimately destroy us. The clarity for what you should choose at this moment hopefully is, well…clear.

week four

APPLICATION

Every morning we wake up with the blessing of a new day. His mercies are new and we can walk in them. Where will we go? What will we do? What will we say? Who will we serve? Before us is a journey that, while often not easy, can be amazingly joyful and filled with purpose. The choices we make define us for a lifetime. Choose the team that wins. Follow the Coach that wrote the book. Follow the Savior that saved your soul. Choose Jesus.

PRAYER

Heavenly Father,

Help me to choose Jesus. May I see the blessings of serving You and not being bound by sin. The enemy wants nothing but to destroy me. Your desire for me is to glorify You, be a blessing to others and change a world. Give me the strength to push away temptation so I won't begin to try to justify the wrong and serve two masters. You are the only true Master of everything, the Beginning and the End, the Alpha and Omega. I praise Your Holy Name and choose to follow and serve You.

I love You, Father. In Jesus' name I pray. Amen.

FAST THIS WEEK

What will you remove this week from the rec room of your life so that you might better focus your heart and mind on God?

We live in a world filled with extracurricular activities. Sports, band, clubs, professional organizations, and opportunities abound for us to fill our time with superfluous activity that doesn't add real value to you or anyone else. Evaluate your recreational activities. Do sports, band, or other forms of entertainment distract you from serving others or worshiping God? Each day this week, set aside a leisure activity. Use the time to be with family, volunteer in your community, or spend unhurried time in Scripture.

For those activities that seem necessary, like sports practices, band rehearsals, etc., make a list of the people who will participate with you. Pray for them each day and look for ways to encourage them to experience life in Christ.

WITH YOUR FAMILY

Before doing this activity with your kids, you try it first. You will need a small tupperware container, a rock (can't be larger than container), and rice. Place the rock in the container and then add rice around the rock until the container is filled so the lid can shut. Take the rice and rock out. Reverse the order. This time put the rice in first then the rock. Were you able to close the lid this time?

CHRIST FIRST, EVERYTHING ELSE SECOND

- Why did everything fit on our first try but not on our second?

- If the container was our day, what do you think the rock represents? (God)

- The rice represents all the other things in our life. What are examples for you?

- How can we make Christ first?

- Read John 3:30. Discuss.

notes

THIS WEEK'S MEMORY VERSE

""Do not let any unwholesome talk come out of your mouths, but only what is helpful for building others up according to their needs, that it may benefit those who listen. And do not grieve the Holy Spirit of God, with whom you were sealed for the day of redemption."

Ephesians 4:29 - 30

SCRIPTURE

Read Ephesians 4

Focus -

"Do not let any unwholesome talk come out of your mouths, but only what is helpful for building others up according to their needs, that it may benefit those who listen. And do not grieve the Holy Spirit of God, with whom you were sealed for the day of redemption."

Ephesians 4:29 - 30

OBSERVATION

So many times we forget the Lord is always with us. It's an obvious truth seen in what we say, how we act, and the shame we feel for our choices. It's difficult to think about what the Lord has seen us do and heard us say. His mercy, grace, and forgiveness stretches far beyond our sinful choices. He has sealed us! As long as He decides to leave us on the Earth, let us be purposeful and careful not to grieve Him, but bless His heart.

week four

APPLICATION

What brings joy to Your heart, Lord? This is a great question to ask. It is amazing what happens when we seek to bless the Lord. We get blessed in return. Make a conscious effort everyday to choose Jesus. He will always be faithful to guide and direct your path. The last thing we should desire is to grieve the One that loves us so. We must do everything we can to find out what He desires of us. Read His word. Pray without ceasing. Follow His lead. We will all be blessed by being a blessing when we choose Jesus.

PRAYER

Heavenly Father,

Help me to choose Jesus. May I desire to bless others and bless You. Give me the strength to do what's right, say what's right, and think what's right so I don't grieve You. Thank You so much for sealing me and keeping me. Your power and might are unexplainable. Lead me and guide me to truth so I may purposefully choose Jesus.

I love You, Father. In Jesus' name I pray. Amen.

FAST THIS WEEK

What will you remove this week from the rec room of your life so that you might better focus your heart and mind on God?

We live in a world filled with extracurricular activities. Sports, band, clubs, professional organizations, and opportunities abound for us to fill our time with superfluous activity that doesn't add real value to you or anyone else. Evaluate your recreational activities. Do sports, band, or other forms of entertainment distract you from serving others or worshiping God? Each day this week, set aside a leisure activity. Use the time to be with family, volunteer in your community, or spend unhurried time in Scripture.

For those activities that seem necessary, like sports practices, band rehearsals, etc., make a list of the people who will participate with you. Pray for them each day and look for ways to encourage them to experience life in Christ.

WITH YOUR FAMILY

This activity requires no materials. Simply take turns giving each other compliments. The trick is, you cannot smirk or smile. You must keep a straight face. The first one to smile loses. Take turns and be creative with your compliments!

BUILD UP

- How did that make you feel?

- How did it make others feel?

- Read Ephesians 4:29-30 and discuss.

- Why should we build each other up?

- When we choose not to use kind words, does it hurt God? Why?

notes

THIS WEEK'S MEMORY VERSE

""Do not let any unwholesome talk come out of your mouths, but only what is helpful for building others up according to their needs, that it may benefit those who listen. And do not grieve the Holy Spirit of God, with whom you were sealed for the day of redemption."

Ephesians 4:29 - 30

SCRIPTURE

Read Acts 3

Focus -

"Repent, then, and turn to God, so that your sins may be wiped out, that times of refreshing may come from the Lord."

Acts 3:19

OBSERVATION

The only good thing about sin is that it can be forgiven. The Lord has given us the wonderful opportunity to be refreshed in our weaknesses. Those times we fail and fall into temptation, He is right there, willing to forgive and pick us up. When we ask for forgiveness, the Lord is always faithful to show us mercy and grace and forgive us of our unrighteous acts against Him. He demonstrates His love and gives us a time of refreshing. He pours purpose into our hearts and gives us the strength to act with boldness and carry out that purpose. What a wonderful Savior and mighty God we serve!

week four

APPLICATION

When we sin, and we will, the conviction from the Holy Spirit that lives within drives us to repent. We must run to the Lord. His desire is to have an intimate relationship with us.

Wow! The Almighty Creator of the Universe wants a relationship with you! Just had to say that again. Our sin will blind us for a time, but if we are His, He will call out to us and we must listen. Falling to our knees and asking for forgiveness is a must if we want to stay close to the One who holds us so tenderly in our times of distress. Praise Him! Ask for forgiveness. Talk with Him. Tell Him your desires. He is listening.

PRAYER

Heavenly Father,

Help me to choose Jesus. Thank You for being so willing to forgive me when I fail You. Please continue to show me how I can be better for You. As I seek Your face, let me understand the freedom that comes from doing what is right and living in truth. Please give me a time of refreshing that can only come from Your Spirit. Continue to mold me into what You need me to be for Your kingdom.

I love You, Father. In Jesus' name I pray. Amen.

FAST THIS WEEK

What will you remove this week from the rec room of your life so that you might better focus your heart and mind on God?

We live in a world filled with extracurricular activities. Sports, band, clubs, professional organizations, and opportunities abound for us to fill our time with superfluous activity that doesn't add real value to you or anyone else. Evaluate your recreational activities. Do sports, band, or other forms of entertainment distract you from serving others or worshiping God? Each day this week, set aside a leisure activity. Use the time to be with family, volunteer in your community, or spend unhurried time in Scripture.

For those activities that seem necessary, like sports practices, band rehearsals, etc., make a list of the people who will participate with you. Pray for them each day and look for ways to encourage them to experience life in Christ.

WITH YOUR FAMILY

This activity requires a shallow plate, colored water, a penny, a tea light candle, and an empty jar. Pour the colored water on the plate. Place the candle in the middle and the penny between the edge of the plate and the middle. Explain that the candle represents God and the penny is sin. We are the water and the jar is forgiveness. Light the candle. Place the jar over the candle. (As the candle goes out it will create a vacuum and pull all the water near to the candle away from the penny.)

DRAW US CLOSE

- Read 1 John 1:9. Why do we need God's forgiveness?
- What must we do to receive God's forgiveness?
- Are you distant from God?
- What do you need to confess to God?
- Take time as a family in silent prayer talking to God.

notes

THIS WEEK'S MEMORY VERSE

""Do not let any unwholesome talk come out of your mouths, but only what is helpful for building others up according to their needs, that it may benefit those who listen. And do not grieve the Holy Spirit of God, with whom you were sealed for the day of redemption."

Ephesians 4:29 - 30

SCRIPTURE

Read Psalm 100

Focus -

"Worship the Lord with gladness, come before Him with joyful songs."

Psalm 100:2

OBSERVATION

Nothing can compare to being right with the Lord. He pulls us close and loves us in a way that is indescribable. When our hearts are tender to His words, we can't help but praise Him with all that is in us. In fact, there's no way to keep it in. It pours out of us like a waterfall spilling into the lives of those around us. Our "quiet times" are more refreshing. Our prayer life doesn't seem boring. Our lives seem manageable because we confess we aren't really in control. He is, and always has been. This is the joyful song we sing as we worship Him with our lives.

APPLICATION

Seek the Lord and He will be found. Give thanks in all things and pursue righteousness. Sing to Him often. (Even if you can't sing; He doesn't care what You sound like.) The joy of being right with your Savior is matchless. He will laugh with you, cry with you, and give you everything you need to live a life that is pleasing to Him. It's far better than sinning for a season. This is a lifetime of peace. Choose Jesus.

PRAYER

Heavenly Father,

Help me to choose Jesus. When I come before You to praise Your Holy Name, please hear me and receive me into Your presence. I acknowledge that You are the All-Powerful Creator of everything. I humbly ask You to show us the pathway of righteousness and give us the boldness to pursue it. I desire to please You. May Your strength be mine as I live my life in a fallen world. I need You.

I love You, Father. In Jesus' name I pray. Amen.

FAST THIS WEEK

What will you remove this week from the rec room of your life so that you might better focus your heart and mind on God?

We live in a world filled with extracurricular activities. Sports, band, clubs, professional organizations, and opportunities abound for us to fill our time with superfluous activity that doesn't add real value to you or anyone else. Evaluate your recreational activities. Do sports, band, or other forms of entertainment distract you from serving others or worshiping God? Each day this week, set aside a leisure activity. Use the time to be with family, volunteer in your community, or spend unhurried time in Scripture.

For those activities that seem necessary, like sports practices, band rehearsals, etc., make a list of the people who will participate with you. Pray for them each day and look for ways to encourage them to experience life in Christ.

WITH YOUR FAMILY

Sometimes when we think about singing praises to God, we worry about if we like the song or if we have a good singing voice. Worship isn't about us. That's the problem. Let's work today as a family to place our focus on God.

WORSHIP

- Read Psalm 100:1-5

- What are some things we know to be true about God?

For example:

- He created everything and everyone.

- He never leaves us even though we might feel alone.

- He loves us forever and demonstrates His love for us.

- He has great power and not even Satan is stronger than Him.

- He sees everything and nothing can be hidden from Him.

- What is a song that you like to sing to praise God? Sing a verse or song together.

notes

week five

THE HALL CLOSET

One day I found Jesus waiting for me at the door. An arresting look was in His eye. As I entered, He said to me, "There is a peculiar odor in the house. There is something dead around here. It's upstairs. I think it is in the hall closet."

As soon as He said this, I knew what He was talking about. Yes, there was a small closet up there on the landing, just a few feet square. In that closet, behind lock and key, I had one or two little personal things that I did not want anyone to know about. Certainly, I did not want Christ to see them. I knew they were dead and rotting things left over from my old life. And yet I loved them, and I wanted them so for myself that I was afraid to admit they were there.

Reluctantly, I went up with Him. As we mounted the stairs the odor became stronger and stronger. He pointed at the door. "It's in there!" I was angry. That's the only way I can put it. I had given Him access to the study, the dining room, the living room, the work room, the playroom, and now He was asking me about a little two-by-four closet. I said to myself, "This is too much. I am not going to give Him the key."

"Well," He said, reading my thoughts, "if you think I'm going to stay up here on the second floor with this odor, you are mistaken. I will take my bed out on the back porch. Then I saw Him start down the stairs. When you have come to know and love Christ, the worst thing that can happen is to sense His fellowship retreat from you. I had to surrender. "I'll give You the key," I said sadly, "but You'll have to open the closet and clean it out. I haven't the strength to do it."

"I know," He said. "I know you haven't. Just give me the key. Authorize Me to take care of that closet and I will."

With trembling hands I passed the key to Him. He took it, walked over to the door, opened it, entered it, took out all the putrefying stuff that was rotting there, and threw it away. Then He cleaned the closet and painted it. It was all done in a moment's time. Oh, what victory and release to have that dead thing out of my life!

FAST THIS WEEK

What will you remove this week from the hall closet of your life so that you might better focus your heart and mind on God?

The hall closet represents our deepest, most hidden sins and temptations. This week's fast isn't something you begin and then end. This week's fast should be the practice that helps you develop a new habit, a God-honoring habit that replaces a sinful habit.

- If gluttony is hidden in your hall closet - fast from food.
- If pride is hidden in your hall closet - fast from self-approval and seeking the approval of others.
- If lust is hidden in your hall closet - fast from media, or those relationships that cause temptation.
- If gossip is hidden in your hall closet - fast from speaking, writing, or reading gossip about others.

What's in your hall closet is uniquely yours. Jesus will forgive. He will help you overcome. Use this week's fast to practice a new habit based on His forgiveness and help.

THIS WEEK'S MEMORY VERSE

"Create in me a clean heart, O God, and renew a right spirit within me. Do not cast me away from Your presence, and do not take Your Holy Spirit from me."

Psalm 51:10 - 11

SCRIPTURE

Read 1 John 4

Focus -

"Love has been perfected among us in this: that we may have boldness in the day of judgment; because as He is, so are we in this world. There is no fear in love; but perfect love casts out fear, because fear involves torment. But he who fears has not been made perfect in love. We love Him because He first loved us."

1 John 4:17 - 19

OBSERVATION

Take time to really consider the first sentence of this passage. "Love has been perfected among us in this: that we may have boldness in the day of judgement, because as He is, so are we in this world."

God's love for you is perfect. Let's be clear. When the Bible says God loves you, it's not in spite of you. It's not the wishful thinking of a star-crossed crush. It's a deep and abiding love that comes from God's choice to create you, to forgive you, to save you, to walk with you through this life and carry you into the next.

When you face the judgment of God you can stand with

week five

boldness, because as Jesus is blameless in this world before the eyes of God - so are you.

Knowing this, believing this, receiving His love, casts out fear. We can freely confess our sin knowing that what comes next isn't judgement, but redemption. We can acknowledge our deepest, darkest secrets before God because His response isn't the critical conviction or disappointment in our utter failure, but the freedom of repentance and the gift of His grace. No matter your secret, regardless of how dark your sin may be, from God, you have nothing to fear, only love and freedom to receive.

APPLICATION

What are you hiding? What are you holding back from God? What are you afraid of?

It's tempting to believe that some things you've done could never possibly be forgiven. But that's not true. Jesus stands ready to forgive your sin. All of it. No matter how dark or secret. Regardless of how long you've held on to it, tried to hide it, or struggled to keep it under control.

Jesus loves you.

Jesus forgives.

Jesus can heal the brokenness and restore what sin has stolen from you.

It begins with confession. Be honest with God today. Open the door to Him that leads to the place of your greatest failure, your deepest hurt, and your darkest secret. When you do, you'll discover the power of His love in your life.

PRAYER

Heavenly Father,

I know You love me. You've told me time and again. You've shown me in numerous ways. And I am grateful for Your love. I don't understand why You love me. I know how many times I've resisted You, rebelled against You and run from You. Yet You love me still. Thank You for loving me. Thank You for Your forgiveness. Give me the courage to face and confess my deepest, darkest, most secret sins to You. Help me to forgive myself and those who have hurt or disappointed me.

I love You, Father. In Jesus' name I pray. Amen.

FAST THIS WEEK

The hall closet represents our deepest, most hidden sins and temptations. This week's fast isn't something you begin and then end. This week's fast should be the practice that helps you develop a new habit, a God-honoring habit that replaces a sinful habit.

- If gluttony is hidden in your hall closet - fast from food.
- If pride is hidden in your hall closet - fast from self-approval and seeking the approval of others.
- If lust is hidden in your hall closet - fast from media, or those relationships that cause temptation.
- If gossip is hidden in your hall closet - fast from speaking, writing, or reading gossip about others.

What's in your hall closet is uniquely yours. Jesus will forgive. He will help you overcome. Use this week's fast to practice a new habit based on His forgiveness and help.

WITH YOUR FAMILY

Use this activity to build team organization. Go to your local dollar store and buy some baskets and tubs. Buy different colors and sizes to meet the needs of your closet. You might give each member of the family a different colored basket/tub. Either tackle this shelf by shelf or take everything out and as a group decide what needs to go back in or what you can donate to a local shelter.

DECLUTTER DELIGHT

- Just like our hall closet gets too full of stuff, how do we get too much stuff in our lives?

- What are some good things in our lives and what are some things we could give up?

- What things did we find in our closet that no one would know about? Why is it wrong to hide things in our lives?

notes

_____

_____

_____

_____

_____

_____

THIS WEEK'S MEMORY VERSE

"Create in me a clean heart, O God, and renew a right spirit within me. Do not cast me away from Your presence, and do not take Your Holy Spirit from me."

Psalm 51:10 - 11

SCRIPTURE

Read Psalm 19

Focus -

"Who can understand his errors? Cleanse me from secret faults. Keep back Your servant also from presumptuous sins; Let them not have dominion over me. Then I shall be blameless, And I shall be innocent of great transgression. Let the words of my mouth and the meditation of my heart be acceptable in Your sight, O Lord, my strength and my Redeemer."

Psalm 19:12 - 14

OBSERVATION

Are you ready to be this honest with yourself? Do you have the courage to pray a bold prayer? The Psalmist was willing to lay it all on the line. He recognized and admitted his weakness. He realized, that even when it felt right, even though he believed he was doing right, that there was potential he was committing presumptuous sins.

He confessed his secret faults, the ones known only to him and God. He willingly invited a Holy God to examine his thoughts, motives, and actions.

week five

APPLICATION

You've heard the saying, "You're only as sick as your secrets." It's true. There's something about secret sin that finds it's way to the surface. Secret sin suffocates your relationship with God, dismantles your relationship with people you care about, and steals the joy from your life. Will you willingly repent of your secret sin and allow God to apply the healing miracle of His grace or will you wait for your secret to be found out?

This is a bold prayer. It takes courage to invite a Holy God to know and forgive those secrets. Rest assured, nothing you confess will surprise God. Everything you confess will be forgiven. And once forgiven, healing begins.

PRAYER

Heavenly Father,

Thank You for Your grace in my life. Thank You for the love and forgiveness You've already given through Jesus. Today, give me the courage to own up to my secret sins. Help me find the humility to recognize and confess my presumptuous sins. I pray Psalm 19:12-14, "Cleanse me from secret faults. Keep back Your servant also from presumptuous sins; Let them not have dominion over me. Then I shall be blameless, and I shall be innocent of great transgression. Let the words of my mouth and the meditation of my heart be acceptable in Your sight, O Lord, my strength and my Redeemer."

I love You, Father. In Jesus' name I pray. Amen.

FAST THIS WEEK

The hall closet represents our deepest, most hidden sins and temptations. This week's fast isn't something you begin and then end. This week's fast should be the practice that helps you develop a new habit, a God-honoring habit that replaces a sinful habit.

- If gluttony is hidden in your hall closet - fast from food.
- If pride is hidden in your hall closet - fast from self-approval and seeking the approval of others.
- If lust is hidden in your hall closet - fast from media, or those relationships that cause temptation.
- If gossip is hidden in your hall closet - fast from speaking, writing, or reading gossip about others.

What's in your hall closet is uniquely yours. Jesus will forgive. He will help you overcome. Use this week's fast to practice a new habit based on His forgiveness and help.

WITH YOUR FAMILY

Use this fun activity to explore your home and yard. Before this activity begins, choose some areas in your home where your family is least likely to visit. You will write out clues to find these places. It all begins in the Hall Closet, where you place the first clue.

For example: It's sometimes high, sometimes low, but regardless it is where our water goes. Down through the hole, into the dark, you will often find in my curve a place where food goes to hide. It's the pipe under the kitchen sink, here you place the next clue.

HALL CLOSET HUNT

- On your quest, what unexpected things did you find?

- Did you find anything that could be dangerous?

- How can you protect yourself and others from dangerous things in your home or life?

notes

_____

_____

_____

_____

_____

_____

_____

_____

_____

_____

_____

_____

_____

_____

THIS WEEK'S MEMORY VERSE

"Create in me a clean heart, O God, and renew a right spirit within me. Do not cast me away from Your presence, and do not take Your Holy Spirit from me."

Psalm 51:10 - 11

SCRIPTURE

Read Ephesians 5

Focus -

"For you were once darkness, but now you are light in the Lord. Walk as children of light (for the fruit of the Spirit is in all goodness, righteousness, and truth), finding out what is acceptable to the Lord. And have no fellowship with the unfruitful works of darkness, but rather expose them."

Ephesians 5:8 - 11

OBSERVATION

Think about your story. Remember where you came from. There was a time before you placed your faith in Christ. Do you remember? Even if you grew up in church, part of your life was spent in darkness. But this verse reveals more. It's not simply that you were in darkness.

You *were* the darkness.

But the love of God has transformed you. Now, you are light in the Lord. As light, you can expose those works of darkness, those fruitless, pointless, wastes of time, effort and energy. God can reveal and you can overcome those hurts, habits, and hang ups that slow you down, drag you down, cause you shame, or cause you pain. You are light in the Lord. Walk as children of light.

week five

APPLICATION

Is there a part of your life where it seems light never shines? Is there something you're holding back from God? Is it a past decision, a source of pain or shame? Is it a current circumstance, an ongoing temptation you can't seem to overcome? Is it a future desire, an ungodly pursuit of an unworthy goal?

As a believer in Jesus Christ, you are light in the Lord. You walk as children of light and that light can shine into the darkest regions of your soul. You may fear what it finds, but that fear is misplaced. Every sin has been forgiven because Jesus died on the cross and rose from the dead. You are free.

As His light shines into your life, quickly confess what it reveals and receive the freedom of forgiveness.

PRAYER

Heavenly Father,

I'll confess, I'm afraid to let go. There are certain temptations I give in to because I can't think of any other way around them. Shine your light into my heart and mind. Help me to see and face the sin I'm unwilling to recognize. Give me the wisdom and courage to overcome the temptation that traps me. Forgive my sin and help me let go. Thank You for the way Your love and grace gently draw me to You. Let the light You've placed in me so shine before men that they may see my good works and glorify You in heaven.

I love You, Father. In Jesus' name I pray. Amen.

FAST THIS WEEK

The hall closet represents our deepest, most hidden sins and temptations. This week's fast isn't something you begin and then end. This week's fast should be the practice that helps you develop a new habit, a God-honoring habit that replaces a sinful habit.

- If gluttony is hidden in your hall closet - fast from food.
- If pride is hidden in your hall closet - fast from self-approval and seeking the approval of others.
- If lust is hidden in your hall closet - fast from media, or those relationships that cause temptation.
- If gossip is hidden in your hall closet - fast from speaking, writing, or reading gossip about others.

What's in your hall closet is uniquely yours. Jesus will forgive. He will help you overcome. Use this week's fast to practice a new habit based on His forgiveness and help.

WITH YOUR FAMILY

In your hall closet, place a new game to play as a family. Invite another family from your church that needs to make a small group connection to spend the evening with you.

FUN FAMILY SURPRISE

- What was your favorite part of the evening?
- How were you able to shine the light of Jesus as you played the game?
- How can you pray for the family you invited over?

notes

THIS WEEK'S MEMORY VERSE

"Create in me a clean heart, O God, and renew a right spirit within me. Do not cast me away from Your presence, and do not take Your Holy Spirit from me."

Psalm 51:10 - 11

SCRIPTURE

Read 1 John 1

Focus -

"If we confess our sins, He is faithful and just to forgive our sin and to cleanse us from all unrighteousness."

1 John 1:9

OBSERVATION

What will you confess? Will your confession be general or specific? Will you ask God to forgive some thing or every thing? There's strength in recognizing specific sins, specific temptations. This verse tells us that as we confess, God is both faithful and just to forgive our sin. This tells us something important.

When you confess, you don't have to be afraid.

God is faithful, meaning He will keep His promise to forgive your sin. He won't back down. He won't relent. He won't forget or forsake His promise to you. But it's more than that.

God's forgiveness is just. It's the right thing for Him to do. Not because you deserve His forgiveness, but because the penalty for your sin, the punishment for your every unrighteous thought, or action, has been paid on the cross

week five

at Calvary. Jesus died for your sin and rose from the dead! Confess your sin and be forgiven!

APPLICATION

Make a list. Take time to make a list of sins you commit today, sins you commit regularly. Make a list of the temptations that trip you up. Confess those sins to God.

Over that list write **FORGIVEN** and 1 John 1:9.

Now…destroy the list. Shred it. Burn it. Trash it. Because God has. You are forgiven. You are free.

PRAYER

Heavenly Father,

I confess my sin to You, specifically, generally.

I confess my need for You and my desire to be pleasing to You. Please forgive me. Thank You for Your faithfulness to me and to Your promise to forgive when I confess. When I sin, help me recognize it and confess it quickly. Thank You that Your love and forgiveness for me are just. I pray that I will live today in a way that is worthy of the life, love, and forgiveness You've given to me.

I love You, Father. In Jesus' name I pray. Amen.

FAST THIS WEEK

The hall closet represents our deepest, most hidden sins and temptations. This week's fast isn't something you begin and then end. This week's fast should be the practice that helps you develop a new habit, a God-honoring habit that replaces a sinful habit.

- If gluttony is hidden in your hall closet - fast from food.
- If pride is hidden in your hall closet - fast from self-approval and seeking the approval of others.
- If lust is hidden in your hall closet - fast from media, or those relationships that cause temptation.
- If gossip is hidden in your hall closet - fast from speaking, writing, or reading gossip about others.

What's in your hall closet is uniquely yours. Jesus will forgive. He will help you overcome. Use this week's fast to practice a new habit based on His forgiveness and help.

WITH YOUR FAMILY

Everyone in the family has to choose one item from the hall closet. Come up with a new use for that item and demonstrate it to the family.

HALL CLOSET CREATIONS

2 Corinthians 5:17 says, "If anyone is in Christ, the new creation has come: the old has gone, the new is here."

- How have you taken something old and made it into something new?
- Can you use your new item to tell someone else about Jesus? If so, what would you say?
- Take an invention from someone else in the family and try to convince the rest of the family that you have a better use for the item. What kinds of things could our friends say to try to convince us to follow someone or something other than Jesus?

notes

THIS WEEK'S MEMORY VERSE

"Create in me a clean heart, O God, and renew a right spirit within me. Do not cast me away from Your presence, and do not take Your Holy Spirit from me."

Psalm 51:10 - 11

SCRIPTURE

Read James 4

Focus -

"Therefore submit to God. Resist the devil and he will flee from you. Draw near to God and He will draw near to you. Cleanse your hands, you sinners; and purify your hearts, you double-minded. Lament and mourn and weep! Let your laughter be turned to mourning and your joy to gloom. Humble yourselves in the sight of the Lord and He will lift you up."

James 4:7 - 10

OBSERVATION

Verse 7 starts with the word, "therefore". We need to notice what it's there for. Verse 6 says, "God resists the proud but gives grace to the humble." Something powerful happens when you humble yourself before God, when you open the deepest, darkest closet within your heart and willingly reveal your most intimate, most embarrassing, most shameful secrets to him.

As you submit to God you discover the strength to resist the devil and the devil flees. As his accusations against you are silenced, you notice how close your Heavenly Father has always been. He draws close to you and you are made

week five

abundantly aware of the sin that stains your hands and heart.

You confess.

He forgives.

As you humble yourself before Him, He lifts you up.

APPLICATION

Examine the closet of your heart. What's left to confess? What are you holding back? What sin would you rather hold on to, what shame would you rather bare, what temptation are you unwilling to abandon rather than receive the grace of God and the freedom that comes as He lifts you up?

From what will you fast this week? Will you give up something you love for something you love even more? What will you sacrifice? Will you give more than you think you can afford and trust God to provide?

Identify the temptation. Confess the sin. Draw near to God. He will draw near to you and lift you up.

PRAYER

Heavenly Father,

I submit my thoughts, my choices, my desires, my dreams, my all to You today. When the devil brings his accusations, give me the strength to resist him. When I am accused, when I am tempted, let my knee-jerk reaction be to draw near to You. Thank You for drawing near to me. I confess my sin. I am broken by the wrongs I have done. Humbly, I come to You and ask Your forgiveness.

I love You, Father. In Jesus' name I pray. Amen.

FAST THIS WEEK

The hall closet represents our deepest, most hidden sins and temptations. This week's fast isn't something you begin and then end. This week's fast should be the practice that helps you develop a new habit, a God-honoring habit that replaces a sinful habit.

- If gluttony is hidden in your hall closet - fast from food.
- If pride is hidden in your hall closet - fast from self-approval and seeking the approval of others.
- If lust is hidden in your hall closet - fast from media, or those relationships that cause temptation.
- If gossip is hidden in your hall closet - fast from speaking, writing, or reading gossip about others.

What's in your hall closet is uniquely yours. Jesus will forgive. He will help you overcome. Use this week's fast to practice a new habit based on His forgiveness and help.

WITH YOUR FAMILY

Invite another family to your home and set up an auction for items in your hall closet. Give family members and friends play money and let them draw for a number to bid on items. Everyone has a chance to bid on what they think should stay in the closet. If you know someone who is actually an auctioneer, invite them over to join in the fun!

HALL CLOSET AUCTION

- How did you feel when someone tried to out-bid you for something you really thought should stay in the closet?

- Did you feel that they didn't really understand why the item was so important to you?

- Why do we place value on one item and not another?

- Does God find great value in you?

- Is God's love for you based on the value someone else puts on you?

- How do you know that Jesus loves you?

notes

week six

TRANSFER THE TITLE

A thought came to me. "Lord, is there any chance that You would take over the management of the whole house and operate it for me as You did that closet? Would You take the responsibility to keep my life what it ought to be?"

His face lit up as He replied, "I'd love to! That is what I want to do. You cannot be a victorious Christian in your own strength. Let Me do it through you and for you. That is the way. "But." He added slowly, "I am just a guest. I have no authority to proceed, since the property is not Mine."

Dropping to my knees, I said, "Lord, You have been a guest and I have been the host. From now on I am going to be the servant. You are going to be the Owner and Master." Running as fast as I could to the strongbox, I took the title deed to the house describing its assets and liabilities, location and situation. I eagerly signed the house over to Him alone for time and eternity. "Here," I said. "Here it is, all that I am and all that I have, forever. Now You can run the house. I'll just remain with You as a servant and friend."

Things are different since Jesus Christ has settled down and made His home in my heart.

FAST THIS WEEK

What will you remove this week as you transfer the title of your life to Jesus so that you might better focus your heart and mind on God?

This week, deny yourself.

Identify the thing that most distracts you from pursuing a deep and intimate relationship with God. This is your fast this week.

Fasting is a practice that teaches self-control. It allows us to learn, over a short, pre-determined period of time that we really are able to overcome temptation and follow in the footsteps of our Savior. Consider making a habit of fasting. Fast beyond Lent. And allow fasting to become a tool God can use in your life to transform you through the renewing of your mind, will, emotions, and choices.

THIS WEEK'S MEMORY VERSE

"And He said to all, "If anyone would come after Me, let him deny himself and take up his cross daily and follow Me. For whoever would save his life will lose it, but whoever loses his life for My sake will save it."

Luke 9:23 - 24

SCRIPTURE

Read Colossians 1

Focus -

"He is the image of the invisible God, the firstborn over all creation. For everything was created by Him, in heaven and on earth, the visible and the invisible, whether thrones or dominions or rulers or authorities—all things have been created through Him and for Him. He is before all things and by Him all things hold together."

Colossians 1:15 - 17

OBSERVATION

As you continue to process your heart being the home of Christ, this day, the goal is to recognize Christ as Lord of All. This Jesus who came to earth and went to the cross, to do for you the one thing you could not do for yourself; pay the price for your sin. Today, recognize that Christ is not only Savior, but He is also Creator. Look back at Colossians 1:15-17. Pay attention to the word everything. Paul points out that everything was created by Him. Not some things but everything! Not only is everything created by Him but Christ

week six

holds everything together. That is true in the world and in your life.

APPLICATION

Take time to consider Christ as Creator. When you go outside today, look around at His creation and imagine what it was like when Christ was creating all that you see. As you look at His creation, think through how He is currently creating you. Take a piece of paper or your journal and list all the ways Christ is making you into His image. Try to write as many as you can. Also, pay attention to Colossians 1:17. "He is before all things and by Him all things hold together." How is Christ holding you together right now?

PRAYER

Heavenly Father,

Thank You for remaining close to me. You are not a Creator who is distant. You are The One True God who stays involved in the details of my life. Thank You for being present in my life.

I love You, Father. In Jesus' name I pray. Amen.

 FAST THIS WEEK

This week, deny yourself.

Identify the thing that most distracts you from pursuing a deep and intimate relationship with God. This is your fast this week.

Fasting is a practice that teaches self-control. It allows us to learn, over a short, pre-determined

period of time that we really are able to overcome temptation and follow in the footsteps of our Savior. Consider making a habit of fasting. Fast beyond Lent. And allow fasting to become a tool God can use in your life to transform you through the renewing of your mind, will, emotions, and choices.

WITH YOUR FAMILY

Gather your family and give each person a container of Play-Doh. Tell them they have five minutes to create something. When time runs out, go around and have each person describe what they created. Have each person sit by their creation as you ask the following questions.

WHO'S IN CHARGE?

- Who is in charge of your Play-Doh creation? (You are!) Why? (Because I created it.)

- Who created you? (God.)

- So, who is in charge of you? (God is.)

- Describe a time when it was hard to recognize that God was in charge.

So often we look at the God who created us and try to ignore the fact that He is in charge of our lives. This week we are going to look more closely at how we can allow God to truly be in charge of every part of our lives.

notes

THIS WEEK'S MEMORY VERSE

"And He said to all, "If anyone would come after Me, let him deny himself and take up his cross daily and follow Me. For whoever would save his life will lose it, but whoever loses his life for My sake will save it."

Luke 9:23 - 24

SCRIPTURE

Read 1 Peter 3

Focus -

"...but in your hearts honor Christ the Lord as holy, always being prepared to make a defense to anyone who asks you for a reason for the hope that is in you; yet do it with gentleness and respect..."

1 Peter 3:15

OBSERVATION

From the very moment of salvation, we not only recognize our need of a Savior, but we also come to understand our need to make Jesus the Lord of our lives. When Jesus saved us, He changed us from the inside out. In that moment, there is a transfer of title. We call that a change of heart. When a person has a change of heart, there is a noticeable difference everywhere else. The heart describes the core of a person. The heart describes the driving force of a person's life. In this passage, Peter reminds us that we are to set apart Christ as Lord, as the primary influencer. Once this takes place, you are ready to represent Jesus everywhere

week six

you go. In fact, when Jesus is Lord, it is evident to everyone around you. Therefore, you will be ready to give an answer to all who notice and ask you to give a reason for the hope you have.

APPLICATION

When was the last time someone noticed your faith and asked you about it? I Peter 3:15 helps us see that this should be a normal occurrence in your life. When Jesus is Lord of you, it should be evident, not only in the schedule you keep, but more importantly, it should be evident in the way you interact with your family, conduct your business, and even in the way you play. Living as a person with a transferred title gives off evidence to whose you are. Do you represent Christ by the way you live? Is He truly the Lord of your life?

PRAYER

Heavenly Father,

Convict me of sin in my life. Help me to be a person who has a walk that matches my talk. Use me in the life of someone else today.

I love You, Father. In Jesus' name I pray. Amen.

FAST THIS WEEK

This week, deny yourself.

Identify the thing that most distracts you from pursuing a deep and intimate relationship with God. This is your fast this week.

Fasting is a practice that teaches self-control. It allows us to learn, over a short, pre-determined

period of time that we really are able to overcome temptation and follow in the footsteps of our Savior. Consider making a habit of fasting. Fast beyond Lent. And allow fasting to become a tool God can use in your life to transform you through the renewing of your mind, will, emotions, and choices.

WITH YOUR FAMILY

Have each member of your family get a partner. Have the partners sit down on the floor, facing each other. Tell them to choose which person is going to be the leader first, and who is going to be the follower. When you say go, the follower must mirror everything that the leader does. Play this for a few rounds, then ask the following questions.

REFLECTIONS

- As the follower, what was your job? (To mirror everything that the leader did.)

- Would you say that the goal of the game is to make it look like you are the same person? (Yes.)

- God calls us to follow Him in such a way that when people see us, they see the reflection of Christ. When we follow Him closely, people can tell that we are allowing someone else to be in charge of our lives.

- Were there times in the game when it was hard to follow the leader? Why?

- Describe a time in your life when it was hard to be a reflection of Christ.

Pray. Ask God to help you to reflect Christ in everything that you do.

notes

THIS WEEK'S MEMORY VERSE

"And He said to all, "If anyone would come after Me, let him deny himself and take up his cross daily and follow Me. For whoever would save his life will lose it, but whoever loses his life for My sake will save it."

Luke 9:23 - 24

SCRIPTURE

Read Romans 10

Focus -

"But what does it say? "The word is near you, in your mouth and in your heart" (that is, the word of faith that we proclaim); because, if you confess with your mouth that Jesus is Lord and believe in your heart that God raised him from the dead, you will be saved. For with the heart one believes and is justified, and with the mouth one confesses and is saved."

Romans 10:9 - 10

OBSERVATION

"Jesus is Lord," is one of the most radical concepts of Christianity. When you make the claim that Jesus is Lord, you are saying that He is not just the Supreme Ruler over ALL, He is also your ruler as well. Jesus was amazingly chosen to come to earth in a miraculous way. Upon coming, he powerfully destroyed the works of the devil and restored our personal connection to God. When Jesus came to earth, He obeyed everything the Father told Him to do. When Jesus left the earth He gave His followers the same task He had

week six

received from the Father - Go reconcile the human family to the Father, destroy the works of the devil, and restore that which was lost. Proclaiming Jesus as Lord means we are to obey what He commands us to do. You are not saved to go to heaven, You are saved to bring heaven to the earth.

APPLICATION

God has placed you in the lives of people who are not connected to Christ or His people. Today, take a bold step. Tell someone about Him and then invite them to attend church with you. People are amazingly open to an invitation from someone they know. It may surprise you, but there is someone near you who will come, if only you ask. Identify them today. Take the time to invest in their lives. Invite them to church with you.

PRAYER

Heavenly Father,

Help me to be bold and speak up about You. I ask You to be the Lord of my life and pray that You would direct my steps and work in and through me.

I love You, Father. In Jesus' name I pray. Amen.

FAST THIS WEEK

This week, deny yourself.

Identify the thing that most distracts you from pursuing a deep and intimate relationship with God. This is your fast this week.

Fasting is a practice that teaches self-control. It allows us to learn, over a short, pre-determined

period of time that we really are able to overcome temptation and follow in the footsteps of our Savior. Consider making a habit of fasting. Fast beyond Lent. And allow fasting to become a tool God can use in your life to transform you through the renewing of your mind, will, emotions, and choices.

WITH YOUR FAMILY

Take some chairs from around your house and play musical chairs. Place one less chair per person in a circle. When you start the music, have the players walk around the chairs. When the music stops, everyone rushes to sit in a chair. Whoever is left without a chair is out. Remove a chair and play again until you have one winner.

MUSICAL CHAIRS

- Did anyone get into a fight over a chair? What did you do?

- Why did you so badly want the chair?

- If these chairs represent the throne of our hearts, do we ever fight with Jesus over who is in control?

- Did anyone get hurt fighting for a chair?

- What area of your life do you need to give over full control to God?

notes

THIS WEEK'S MEMORY VERSE

"And He said to all, "If anyone would come after Me, let him deny himself and take up his cross daily and follow Me. For whoever would save his life will lose it, but whoever loses his life for My sake will save it."

Luke 9:23 - 24

SCRIPTURE

Read Galatians 2

Focus -

"I have been crucified with Christ. It is no longer I who live, but Christ who lives in me. And the life I now live in the flesh I live by faith in the Son of God, who loved me and gave Himself for me."

Galatians 2:20

OBSERVATION

Lordship means your heart has become Christ's home. Take this moment to think about the Crucifixion of Jesus. Think about God in the flesh being struck with whips by Roman soldiers. Remember the people that mocked Him and spit on Him. Think about Roman soldiers placing a crown of thorns on His head and laughing in His face. Remember the people who gathered to watch Him as Soldiers nailed His hands and feet to the cross. Remember the two thieves on each side of Jesus getting what they deserved, all the while Jesus willingly allows Himself to be crucified. This is the One who loved you and gave Himself for you. Remember, like Paul, you too were crucified with Christ. Now, you no longer

week six

live, but Christ lives in you. Live today by faith in the Son of God.

APPLICATION

Read these words out loud. Listen to the sound of your voice as you read them:

I'm the one who spat upon the Savior. I'm the one who mocked His Holy Name.

I'm the one who said with all the rest, "Crucify Him!" I'm the one. I'm the one to blame!

I'm the one who made Him go to Calvary. I'm the one who nailed Him to the tree!

Even though I am the one who brought all this on Him, He's the One Who tells me He forgives me!

What kind of Man is this? Why does He care for me?

Look what I've done to Him! I guess He doesn't see.

That I'm the one to blame.

I caused Him all this shame!

What kind of Man is this?

Truly this was the Son of God!

I should have been the one to die!

What greater love has anyone than this,

That He would give Himself for such as I!

PRAYER

Heavenly Father,

Today, I want to remember the sacrifice You made for me on the cross. Speak to me through Your word and my experiences with You this week. Help me never forget the price You paid on the cross for me and my sins.

I love You, Father. In Jesus' name I pray. Amen.

FAST THIS WEEK

This week, deny yourself.

Identify the thing that most distracts you from pursuing a deep and intimate relationship with God. This is your fast this week.

Fasting is a practice that teaches self-control. It allows us to learn, over a short, pre-determined period of time that we really are able to overcome temptation and follow in the footsteps of our Savior. Consider making a habit of fasting. Fast beyond Lent. And allow fasting to become a tool God can use in your life to transform you through the renewing of your mind, will, emotions, and choices.

WITH YOUR FAMILY

BATTLE FOR THE THRONE

Mark a big circle on the floor and place a chair in the middle (you can make the circle with toilet paper, chalk, tape, etc).

SAY: Let's pretend like this circle is your heart and this chair represents the throne of your heart. Who sits on a throne? (A king, the person in charge.)

SAY: When Jesus became the boss of your life, you committed that you want Him to be in charge. In other words, you want Him to sit on the throne. (Place a cross on the chair.)

- Are there times we try to take back

control?

Have someone pick up the cross and place it on the floor inside the circle. Have that child sit in the chair. This demonstrates how we sometimes try to take charge of our lives. Be sure to point out that Jesus doesn't leave. We can't lose our salvation, even when we try to take control of our own lives.

- Do you think it's a good thing or a bad thing when we take control of our own lives? Why?
- What is one area of your life that you need to ask God to help you give up control?

notes

THIS WEEK'S MEMORY VERSE

"And He said to all, "If anyone would come after Me, let him deny himself and take up his cross daily and follow Me. For whoever would save his life will lose it, but whoever loses his life for My sake will save it."

Luke 9:23 - 24

SCRIPTURE

Read Luke 9

Focus -

"And He said to all, "If anyone would come after Me, let him deny himself and take up his cross daily and follow Me. For whoever would save his life will lose it, but whoever loses his life for My sake will save it."

Luke 9:23 - 24

OBSERVATION

From a description of His own fate, Jesus describes the responsibility of His followers. As dreadful as this destiny might be, those who choose to follow Him may expect nothing other than the opposition that is the trademark for followers of Jesus. In this proclamation, Jesus is not some sort of masochist who embraces suffering. On the contrary, without reservation, Jesus commits to the purpose of God. Because of this commitment, there is resistance from this world.

Just like Christ, believers are called to fulfill God's plan. In this pursuit we will encounter hostility and even the experience of great suffering should be expected. To take

week six

up the cross, in its Roman context, would have referred literally to the victim's carrying the crossbeam of the cross from the site of sentencing to the place of crucifixion.

APPLICATION

Take the time to remember the passion of Christ in the last few hours of His life. Consider Christ's experience on the cross. Recognize that God has called and equipped you to follow in His steps. Every day, you are called to walk with Jesus. Follow Him daily. Walk with Him today. Do not be afraid to lose your life for His sake. In doing so, you will begin to really live.

PRAYER

Heavenly Father,

I willingly choose to follow You today. Help me deny my selfish desires, my sinful tendencies and live every day faithfully embracing Your will, Your Word, and Your plan for my life. Speak to me through the passion of Christ. Help me understand what it means to carry my cross.

I love You, Father. In Jesus' name I pray. Amen.

FAST THIS WEEK

This week, deny yourself.

Identify the thing that most distracts you from pursuing a deep and intimate relationship with God. This is your fast this week.

Fasting is a practice that teaches self-control. It allows us to learn, over a short, pre-determined period of time that we really are able to overcome temptation and follow in the footsteps of our Savior. Consider making a habit of fasting. Fast beyond Lent. And allow fasting to become a tool God can use in your life to transform you through the renewing of your mind, will, emotions, and choices.

WITH YOUR FAMILY

Hide an object in the house. Tell your family that their job is to find the object. However, there's a catch. They must look for it with their eyes closed. Give them a few minutes to find the item. (They won't be able to.) Try it again, only this time you will tell them where to go. Use your words to help them find the object.

FOLLOW MY VOICE

- Was it easier to find the item with or without my help?

- How did you find the item when I gave you instructions? (By obeying what you said.)

- Were there times you doubted me while we were playing? Did you want to do things your own way?

- If you ignored me and just tried to find the prize on your own, would it have taken you longer or shorter? (Longer. Or I might not have found it at all!)

SAY: As Christians, we want Jesus to be in charge of our lives. But sometimes we try to ignore what He wants. That's when we struggle or get into trouble. If we obey Him, one day at a time, He will help us to live lives focused on Him.

notes